The American Men of Letters Series

WALT WHITMAN

Reconsidered

RICHARD
CHASE

 William Sloane Associates, Inc.
Publishers, New York

To Lionel Trilling

Parts of Chapter I are reprinted from *Leaves of Grass One Hundred Years After*, edited by Milton Hindus, with the permission of the publishers, Stanford University Press. Copyright 1955 by the Board of Trustees of Leland Stanford Junior University.

Published simultaneously in the Dominion of Canada by George J. McLeod Limited, Toronto.

Printed in the U.S.A.

Library of Congress Catalog Card Number: 55–6326.

CONTENTS

PREFACE

I THINK of this book as an essay in "appreciation," of a cultural-historical sort. Partly because 1955 is the hundredth anniversary of the first edition of *Leaves of Grass*, I have wanted to treat Whitman lovingly and to place him, if possible, where he ought truly to be in our culture and our feelings. So that besides looking fairly directly at his most interesting works, I have spent some time in comparing him with other authors, in seeing him in relation to national attitudes, and to noticing some shifts of opinion about him. But you can't treat a man like Whitman lovingly without offering him considerable opposition, and so if this book is an "appreciation," it is also an attempt at criticism. The critcism, I hope, is specific enough to refer directly to the literary qualities of the poems and essays. But beyond certain comments at the end of the second chapter, I have not attempted, nor would be competent to attempt, the kind of rigorous linguistic analysis which is now practiced by many critics. This is not because I suppose (as some people do) that Whitman's poetry disappears like chaff before the wind when subjected to a rigorous criticism—it seems certain that a considerable body of poetry exists within *Leaves of Grass* and that this poetry will always survive and indeed seem enhanced by critical attacks, of whatever kind and of whatever degree of severity.

Surely we honor Whitman first of all as the supreme poet of American optimism and pragmatism, the rhapsodist of our material and spiritual resources, the unabashed celebrant of the self at home in an open, dynamic universe. Generally speaking, he rests in our historical understanding, as well as in our affections, at the opposite pole from more meticulous artists and more somber moralists, such as Hawthorne and Henry James. In the ensuing pages I have suggested some modifications of this traditional account of our literary history; but at no point do I intend to deny or replace it, believing, as I do, that it is necessary to any realistic view of the matter.

I am acutely aware of the fact that some readers of this book are going to feel that in my attempts at appreciation and criticism, I have unduly scaled down or depreciated the greatness of Whitman. This has certainly not been my intention. I have the greatest admiration for Whitman, both as poet and prophet. And although my approach has forced me to stress on the whole the poet rather than the prophet, I have not failed to understand (as it seems to me) that finally we cannot have the one without the other.

At the same time I have felt, as I know others have, that some of our ways of praising Whitman have not been very discriminating or accurate, that although the public image of Whitman presented to us by his admirers has been imposing, it has seldom been clear.

It is in the name of concreteness and clarity, then, and not from a desire to withhold from Whitman his due, that I have concentrated, in my pages of critical inquiry, on Whitman the comic poet, the radical realist, and the profound elegist. I offer the same reason for having spoken of Whitman's life as something of an ordeal rather than as merely a happy excursion through nineteenth-century America, with a pause now and then for a bracing sexual or mystic experience. My way of looking at Whitman is one way; there are certainly others.

But it is not only the indiscriminate admiration of Whitman I have wanted to question in the ensuing pages. Just as the modern Whitman idolatry descends from the disciples who began to surround Whitman in his Washington period, so there is a powerful body of contemporary opinion which descends from the "genteel" critics who attacked Whitman in his own day. And in writing this book I have been strongly impelled by my sense of the unjustified devaluation Whitman has encountered at the hands of that highly skilled linguistic and symbolistic criticism which exerts so much influence at present, particularly among younger readers. It is hard to assess such things, but I have often felt that now, one hundred years after the first appearance of *Leaves of Grass*, Whitman's reputation, despite what we may say to the contrary in our moments of public piety, is really not very high, that *Leaves of Grass* is not read even as much as it used to be. (Of course it has never been read, and never will be read, by the great democratic audience the author hoped for.) Whitman's reputation is certainly not high among the intelligent students, graduate and undergraduate, whom I meet. And I have been led to my interpretation of Whitman in part by a feeling that because of our rather vague notions about his work we have been in danger of entirely losing sight of what is vital and enduring in this author. Time enough after one has attempted to define Whitman's true, undeniable genius, his residual and authentic power, to ask if in the process of definition one has not at some points underestimated his full greatness or failed to see him in all his aspects at once—so I have thought in writing this book.

I believe also that some readers will think I have concentrated too heavily on "Song of Myself" and granted it too much importance in the Whitman canon. My feeling is, simply, that "Song of Myself" is Whitman's greatest and richest work. But I would point to another impulse which I constantly felt as I considered "Song of Myself." This impulse was to protest what seems to me the period of deformed sensibility we have been living through during the last fifteen years. The taste of the time has been favorable to works that display conservative values—the ideal is a well-made poem (or poetic play or novel) full of symbols which admit a religious interpretation. This mode of taste dictates a preference among Whitman's poems (if for any at all) for "When Lilacs Last in the Dooryard Bloom'd"—here at least, it is said, Whitman was beginning in his crude way to master poetic form. No one will deny that the Lincoln elegy is an exquisite poem. But to prefer it to "Song of Myself" is to prefer, as many people do, *Billy Budd* to *Moby Dick*, *The Cocktail Party* to *The Waste Land*, Hemingway's *The Old Man and the Sea* to *The Sun Also Rises*, Faulkner's *The Bear* to *The Sound and the Fury*, or, for that matter, *The Tempest* to *Hamlet*. The preferences may be justifiable in detail, but the state of mind they reflect is not to be admired, suggesting, as it does, a dislike for writing which arises out of the native energies and dilemmas of life and is committed to the radical literary and cultural values of its time. "Song of Myself" is this kind of writing.

One word about the biographical portions. For the facts I have depended on well-known sources, and the only originality I lay claim to is in some of my formulations of the meaning of these facts. Nor have I aimed at anything like a complete biography. The period of Whitman's life before 1855 will of course always be the most important in the attempt to understand the man and his work. And so I have written on this part of the life of my subject more at length than on any other. Looking over the book as a whole, I think the reader may find certain biographical passages which do not strike him as strictly necessary to the argument or which seem to him too familiar to bear repeating. I would ask this reader simply to leave these pages to readers who may not have in mind even the best known facts about Whitman. Whitman's life, furthermore, is so fas-

cinating in itself that it seems a pity not to include at least
its general outlines in any book about him.

I mention here some of the books to which I feel particu-
larly indebted. Notable among these are Gay Wilson Allen's
Walt Whitman Handbook, Emory Holloway's *Whitman:
an Interpretation in Narrative*, Basil de Selincourt's *Walt
Whitman: A Critical Study*, and Frederik Schyberg's *Walt
Whitman*. I have learned much from F. O. Matthiessen's
American Renaissance and D. H. Lawrence's *Studies in Classic
American Literature*. My book was well advanced before the
appearance of Randall Jarrell's essay called "Walt Whitman:
He Had His Nerve" (now included as "Some Lines from
Whitman" in Jarrell's *Poetry and the Age*), but his essay
struck many responsive chords. Let me mention also Bliss
Perry's early biography *Walt Whitman, His Life and Work*
and Jean Catel's *Walt Whitman: la naissance du poète*. Pro-
fessor Allen's critical biography of Whitman, *The Solitary
Singer*, was published too late for me to consult it.

The text of *Leaves of Grass* which I have used is the standard
one, finally established for all practical purposes in 1882. Since
this is the text that all but specialists read, I have used it on all
occasions, unless otherwise noted, without attention to varia-
tions in earlier editions.

WALT WHITMAN RECONSIDERED

CHAPTER I

BEGINNINGS

THE FIRST THING to admit is that Walt Whitman was different from us. He was a product of those decades just before the Civil War, of the freshness, the large-mindedness, the complex versatility, the general vigor and adventurousness which the war and the Gilded Age did so much to destroy. It is possible, in moods of pessimism and nostalgia, to think that the years between 1820 and 1860 were the best this country is destined to know. But if we do sometimes feel this way, the feeling merely reinforces our sense of the abyss history has made between us and the time of Whitman's youth and early middle-age.

We give over much of our energy to problems generated by modern mass society and the grim, self-lacerating routines within a context of international fear which darken the color of modern life. Many of our problems Whitman, like most people of his time, would hardly understand as problems at all. Our agonized preoccupation with the present is bound to sever some of our connections with the past. But fortunately, when we think of Walt Whitman we can still feel that not all the connections have been cut; whenever we can muster enough of the historical imagination (I would say collective memory, if I could really believe there is such a thing), we feel that it is a *natural* experience to recapture our sense of what Whitman and his works were like.

Perhaps it is the variousness of Whitman's character, its

free multiplicity as contrasted with our sameness or our specialization, that first strikes us as being attractive. We recall that traditionally it was thought that to be various was to be, in an exemplary way, an American. And in this sense Whitman is exemplary—this journeyman printer, newspaper man, schoolteacher, small-time politician, indolent bachelor, satyr, male nurse, mystic, pre-Haldeman-Julius crank, friend of mankind, this humorous loafer, principled bath-taker, saunterer, sage, and author of *Leaves of Grass*. It is the duty of criticism, at any rate, to conceive of Whitman in his diversity, to see in him a wildly paradoxical yet somehow "unitary" man, furtive, visionary, lethargic, witty, stubborn, and possessed of a great poetic talent. Often appearing to accept the identities the world has sought to impose upon him, he finally succeeds in resisting and eluding them. For example, his immediate disciples and many of his readers in later times have called him the good gray poet. He is not the good gray poet, and yet in a way he is, with his benevolent fatherly mildness.

In the 1920's, in his impressive *Three Essays on America*, Van Wyck Brooks understood Whitman to be the "focal center" of the American experience; in the man and his work Brooks saw the national character at last "precipitated" and a massive synthesis of the native realism and vitality with the native spirituality at last achieved. But nowadays, in the light of modern scholarship and criticism, we cannot quite see in Whitman the national norm, because this would mean that we must think of Melville, Hawthorne, and James as eccentric, so different are some of their fundamental attitudes from those of Whitman. This did not seem anomalous to Brooks, but it does to us, to whom history has shown that Melville, Hawthorne, and James also lay claim to centrality in our cultural tradition. We are less certain than Brooks that we shall ever be able to speak with conviction about the "focal center" of American civilization, but we are certain that if we ever do clearly discern such a "center," Whitman will be found to reside there with others very unlike him. We incline to believe that American culture has been more multiform than Brooks wished to understand, that (if we are to keep the terminology at all) there are several "centers" to reckon with, and that if Whitman is normative, so in their ways are others.

Whitman is not quite the fountainhead of realism in fiction and poetry he has often been said to be. He was too much the quirky transcendentalist to be the spiritual father of Theodore Dreiser; yet his influence on him has been considerable. He is not quite the political radical he was thought to be in the 1930's, being on the whole plainly conservative as petty-bourgeois Americans are conservative, and yet his writings are full of inspiring democratic idealism. He is not the stunned and musing savage Santayana thought he was; yet there is something infantile and primitive in the quality of his affections. He is not to be summed up as the strident, "merging" prophet described in D. H. Lawrence's essay (to which I shall return in a moment); yet sometimes he is this prophet. He is not merely the combination of metaphysical wit, Yankee 'cuteness, and nervy lyric poet described in Randall Jarrell's *Poetry and the Age*, being also much committed, even at his most lyric, to great public effects, historical gestures and rhapsodic celebrations.

Whitman is hard to pin down. He resists identities, especially those which disguise the fact that his personality was so considerably indeterminate, neurotic, power conscious, furtive, given alternately to dreams of order and of annihilation and that despite all his absurdities he was a great poet and, in ways open to definition, a profound and salutary revolutionary force in our culture. To remember that Whitman resists identities must be the minimum responsibility of anyone who presumes to write about him.

The voice of criticism nowadays officially maintains—whenever it speaks loosely to a large audience—that Whit-

man's poetry is widely admired and loved. We now easily
tune to his wave length, wrote Henry Seidel Canby at the end
of a biography published in 1943. My own impression is that
this was and is wrong. Whitman's poetry had a measure of
popularity in the twenties, when critics were prophets and
puritans were anathema. But Melville, Hawthorne, and James,
also being discovered in the twenties, have come to outshine
Whitman in the forties and fifties. The radical politics that inspired an admiration for Whitman in the thirties has largely
disappeared, and Whitman's reputation suffered from the general disillusion. At present the taste for poetry, almost to the
extent that it exists, is conditioned by the direct or indirect
influence of Pound, Eliot, and the "new critics." This influence has been salutary in many ways, but unfortunately it
has encouraged a repudiation of Whitman. Most critics of
poetry seem to share Pound's uneasy relation to Whitman as
expressed in his poem called "A Pact," in which the best he
can find to say to his "pig-headed father" is:

> It was you that broke the new wood;
> Now is a time for carving.
> We have one sap and one root—
> Let there be commerce between us.*

Like most modern pacts, this one seems ready to erupt in fresh
hostilities.

For every reader of poetry whose dislike of Whitman stems
from a high ideal of craftsmanship, as in the case of Pound,
there are ten who, if they do not merely reject Whitman because they find his eccentricity, egotism, and sententiousness
odious, launch at him the charge that his moral view is indiscriminate, infantile, ignorant of the tragic dilemmas of life.
Most readers, that is, seem to have been regarding Whitman in

* From *Personae* by Ezra Pound, reprinted with permission of the
publishers, New Directions.

recent years essentially as Lawrence did in his *Studies in Classic American Literature*. The Whitman Lawrence knew was almost exclusively the publicist and prophet—the promulger of strident platitudes, the creature of ego and will, the seer who proclaimed that "I am he that aches with amorous love," but who actually knew no ache that was not abstract and mechanical, the poet who was great in confronting death but mistakenly made of death an ideal, the philosopher who desired so to "merge" with everyone and everything that his view amounts merely to a solipsism and is therefore unreliable as morality. And it was the prophetic Whitman whom Lawrence found great, as well as erroneous—the Whitman who in some unexplained, inadvertent way became the elegist of the self and who opened out a healthy future for mankind by finally delivering the soul from the decadent Christian requirement of salvation and teaching that "the soul is neither 'above' nor 'within'" but "a wayfarer down the open road."

Both in his condemnation and in his praise Lawrence has his point. The merging, solipsistic, stridently abstract prophet is to be heard in nearly all of Whitman's poetry, beginning with "Song of Myself." The moral realist, the liberator who reclaims the soul for the free, vital, naturalistic exploration of the future is not heard so persistently but is indubitably present in "Song of Myself," "Song of the Open Road," and a few other poems. But the limits of Lawrence's general thesis about American literature and, no doubt, the compulsions of his so English and so moralistic protestant temperament lead him to consider Whitman entirely in terms of his prophetic program. Although it is true that we cannot finally have Whitman *without* his prophetic program and do not want him without it, we can nevertheless look at it from the underside, as it were, where the elegist is not only a world prophet but an unsurpassable poet and where the liberator of the soul is not only a preacher but a great comic writer and realist.

For purposes of discrimination, it is useful to speak of Whitman's poetry as opposed to his prophecy. Actually, everything Whitman wrote is prophetic, so that what one wants to do from the literary point of view is to discover where the prophecy is also poetry and where it is not. In *Specimen Days* (1882) there is a discussion of Carlyle, in which Whitman seems to be sizing up himself as well as Carlyle, and one reads there the following: "The word prophecy is much misused; it seems narrow'd to prediction merely. That is not the main sense of the Hebrew word translated 'prophet'; it means one whose mind bubbles up and pours forth as a fountain, from inner, divine spontaneities revealing God. Prediction is a very minor part of prophecy. The great matter is to reveal and outpour the Godlike suggestions pressing for birth in the soul. This is briefly the doctrine of the Friends or Quakers."

It was neither Lawrence's purpose nor his inclination to separate those expressions of Whitman's prophecy which are enlivened by "inner, divine spontaneities" from those which merely predict or prescribe—although, in the above passage, it is obviously Whitman's purpose to insist on this difference. Therefore Lawrence's generalizations need a good deal of qualification before they can be said to apply to Whitman's poetry, and especially to his best poetry. "Song of Myself" and "As I Ebb'd with the Ocean of Life," for example, contain the work of a poet Lawrence did not recognize, the poet who says that his words are "reminders" of

> life untold, and of freedom and extrication,

the poet who can imagine himself walking

> Where the bat flies in the Seventh-month eve, where
>   the great gold-bug drops through the dark,

who says

I fly those flights of a fluid and swallowing soul. . . .
Agonies are one of my changes of garments. . . .
I am the man, I suffer'd, I was there,

who can speak of

> The hiss of the surgeon's knife, the gnawing teeth of
> his saw,
> Wheeze, cluck, swash of falling blood, short wild
> scream, and long, dull, tapering groan,

who strolls along the beaches of "Paumonok," where,

> Fascinated, my eyes reverting from the south, dropt,
> to follow those slender windrows,
> Chaff, straw, splinters of wood, weeds, and the sea-
> gluten.

At his best Whitman is full of irony, wit, and lyric realism. His poems are concerned with particularity, point of view, separation, and doubt. They are written by a poet who does not pretend that he lives in a totally cognizable world, who does not pretend to know himself except by "faint clews and indirections," whose pretensions to know himself are mocked, indeed, by an ironical other self. They are written by a poet who knows, after all, that the people and events around him "are not the me myself" and who carefully stands "both in and out of the game and watching and wondering at it." Surely the poet who wrote "Out of the Cradle Endlessly Rocking" cannot be accused of being ignorant of loneliness, exclusion, and ultimate loss. Death is not an ideal terminus in "Song of Myself" or "Song of the Open Road"—nor in these poems is animality merely cerebral, nor are ego and will unmodulated by genial emotions and sensuous pleasure. "No, Walt, you give yourself away," writes Lawrence, comparing Whitman's "merging" tendencies with physical law. "Matter *does* gravitate, helplessly. But men are tricksy-tricksy, and they shy all sorts of ways." True enough, but Walt Whitman too, both as a poet and as a man, was tricksy-tricksy and shied all sorts of ways, until, that is, he became the Whitman Lawrence knew.

Consider the unknown poet who in the spring of 1855 was revising and editing his first volume of poems. He set the type himself at the printing establishment of Andrew and James Rome in Brooklyn. When the volume was published in July, its readers beheld a thin, dark green quarto containing twelve poems and bearing, on the cover, the ornate curves of gilded lettering which announced, with the help of symbolic grasses and flowers, that the title of the book was *Leaves of Grass*. Although the author did not declare his name in the usual manner, a certain "Walt Whitman" was referred to, in one of the poems, as "an American, one of the roughs, a Kosmos." Interested readers, of whom there were few, might have discovered that the copyright was held by "Walter Whitman." And no reader could miss the portrait, which served as frontispiece, of a bearded man of somewhat indeterminate age, dressed in shirt sleeves and broadbrimmed hat, his dark undershirt visible at the neck, his body carelessly at ease, his extraordinary, heavy-lidded eyes, enigmatic in their indolent introspection. If this man was a kosmos and one of the roughs, he was, it appeared, a somewhat relaxed kosmos and a gentle, distinctly faunlike rough. Whitman printed about a thousand copies of his book and sold almost none. Except for a mixed batch of reviews, the response was limited to a few of the literary men—most notably Emerson—to whom the author hopefully sent his volume. It would be a long time before the world was ready to admit that one of the remarkable books of the nineteenth century had issued from Rome Brothers printing house. But neither the book of poems nor the extraordinary man pictured on the frontispiece had leapt out of the void. They had developed slowly and uncertainly, more so than most poems and poets. In his letter of congratulation to

Whitman, Emerson expressed some inferential curiosity about the "long foreground" which he knew must precede *Leaves of Grass*. It is not my purpose here to present a detailed view of this long foreground but merely to mention some of its representative episodes.

Whitman was born into a declining family which tended in the poet's generation to suffer neurosis, idiocy, poverty, sickness, and hard luck. He was the second of nine children. Of these one brother, Andrew, became a drunkard and, after imposing a slatternly and loose-principled wife on his mother's hospitality, died of tuberculosis at thirty-seven. Another brother, Jesse, contracted syphilis and died after years in an insane asylum. The youngest brother, Eddie, was an imbecile and epileptic. Walt's favorite sister, Hannah, though gifted, became squalid, eccentric, and unbalanced during a long and harrowing marriage to an indigent painter who tried to make an artistic career in Burlington, Vermont, and was given to spells of drunkenness and paranoia. The family life which nourished so much human failure seems to have been characterized in Walt's boyhood by a kind of moral and psychic squalor, anxiety, restlessness, and vagrancy, and there can be no doubt that Whitman's lifelong concern with cleanliness and health, which borders sometimes on the crankish and forms also a part of his prophetic program for democracy, was a response to his family life. The wishful image one remembers from Whitman's newspaper editorials of Manhattan surrounded by thousands of nude, healthy citizens bathing in the rivers is a utopian compensation for the squalor he had known. And the history of his brothers and sisters lends a certain concreteness to the word "sane" in the well-known phrase from "When Lilacs Last in the Dooryard Bloom'd," "O sane and sacred death."

Walt was born on May 31, 1819, at West Hills, Long Island, in the family farmhouse. Walter Whitman, the father, was the first of an extensive family line, which reached back into New England, to leave farming. He became a carpenter, it being his practice to build a house and then move into it until it was sold or lost to creditors. Although the Whitmans do not seem to have lived in actual hardship, they did not live so well as had the earlier generations of the family. These had enjoyed a relatively settled life and had apparently known a good deal of prosperity until, after the Revolution, the family fortunes began gradually to decline. One may doubt if Walter Whitman filled what were later to be his son's prescriptions for ideal American manhood and paternity, invoking as these did a love of comrades, a heroic frame of body and of mind, and a poetic nature. Walter Whitman is said to have been respected as a good workman, but he was generally silent and morose, and sometimes given to outbursts of anger; a photograph makes him appear puzzled and aggrieved. One is not surprised that in Walt's poetry, wherever, as in the *Sea Drift* poems, he is concerned with the metaphysical status of the self, he tends to use paternity as an image of chaos. Apart from his poetry, Walt's attitude toward his father seems to have alternated between affection and indifference. There was at least enough of sympathy between them to allow them to work together at carpentering in the early 1850's, and before the father's death in 1855, Walt took him on a final visit to the countryside and the family homestead.

Whitman got some of his lifelong ideas from his father. Walter Whitman was a convinced Democrat of the Jeffersonian and Jacksonian traditions. And he had affinities even more radical, two of his heroes being Tom Paine and Elias Hicks, the dissident Quaker. He had no religion, beyond a partiality for Quakerism.

Walt's mother gave the family whatever stability and order it had. She was a more admirable person in nearly every way than her husband, and the worship of his mother is of course one of the most striking facts about the poet's life. In *Specimen Days* Whitman recorded his impressions upon revisiting for the first time in more than forty years the scenes of his child-hood (except for the trip with his father mentioned above). In these notes he exhibits that haunting sense of mystery with which he always regarded "the go-befores and embryons," the roots of things. Poking about the old homestead he is mys-tified and reverential. The decaying graves of his ancestors, and indeed the whole scene, he finds, as he keeps saying, "sterile." Yet if there is anything vital among the images his memory resurrects, it is his mother's family, the Van Velsors. Of the Van Velsor homestead he writes, "the whole scene, with what it arous'd, memories of my young days there half a century ago, the vast kitchen and ample fireplace and sitting room adjoining, the plain furniture, the meals, the house full of merry people, my grandmother Amy's sweet old face in its Quaker cap, my grandfather, 'the Major,' jovial, red, stout, with sonorous voice and characteristic physiognomy, with actual sights themselves, made the most pronounc'd half-day's experience of my whole jaunt." Walt Whitman gained from his mother the stubborn perseverance upon which he could count in periods of adversity, and perhaps also an inwardness and sense of mystery. These qualities were confirmed in the mother by her Quaker beliefs and in her son by that strain of Quaker feeling which is observable in him. Despite these sober virtues, however, the Van Velsors were a more various and vivid family than the Whitmans, and Walt records the fact that his "mother, as a young woman, was a daily and daring rider." Still, there was little of vividness, variety, or gaiety in the environment in which Walt himself grew up. The picture of his mother, taken in advancing years, makes her look, with her strong, broad face, somewhat resigned and sad; yet she has an air of triumph, of endurance, of humor, of worldly wisdom. Whitman's description of a family scene in "There Was a

Child Went Forth" strikes one as referring authentically to his own parents:

> The mother at home quietly placing the dishes on the
>   supper-table,
> The mother with mild words, clean her cap and gown,
>   a wholesome odor falling off her person and
>   clothes as she walks by,
> The father, strong, self-sufficient, manly, mean, anger'd,
>   unjust,
> The blow, the quick loud word, the tight bargain, the
>   crafty lure.

There is much evidence, such as the series of touching letters that passed between them in the Civil War period, that the attachment between Walt and his mother was both close and lifelong. The mother was almost illiterate and never understood in the least the poems her son wrote.

But despite the mother's influence, one's general impression of the family life, as I have said, is of laxity and of restless anxiety. As Holloway observed, there was little sense of common purpose or family solidarity. Possibly the influence of this mode of life on the later Whitman is suggested in the lines from "There Was a Child Went Forth" which follow immediately those quoted above:

> The family usages, the language, the company, the
>   furniture, the yearning and swelling heart,
> Affection that will not be gainsay'd, the sense of what
>   is real, the thought if after all it should prove
>   unreal,
> The doubts of day-time and the doubts of night-time,
>   the curious whether and how,
> Whether that which appears so is so, or is it all flashes
>   and specks?

On other occasions too Whitman is accustomed to embark from a reminiscence of his father and mother upon the moral and metaphysical question of what is "real" and what is "unreal." His lifelong concern with "identity" and his many speculations as to how identity can be formed or maintained or eluded may be traced to the unsettled family life of his earliest days.

In 1823 the Whitmans moved to Brooklyn, then a town of seven thousand inhabitants, where the family changed, for several years, from house to house, and Walt began an irregular course of schooling. At one of the Brooklyn public schools Walt was remembered in later years to have been "a big, good-natured lad, clumsy and slovenly in appearance, but not otherwise remarkable." And this is the first of a long series of testimonials to that incorrigible indolence which is one of the salient characteristics of Walt Whitman's temperament and which is in striking contrast to his intermittent capacity for hard work and for brilliant outbursts of energy.

Walt probably left school in 1830 and from then until 1836 was employed at various jobs in and around Brooklyn and New York. We have a glimpse of the awkward, shambling, but handsome youth working as an errand boy in a lawyer's and then a doctor's office, and then learning to set type in the offices of the *Long Island Patriot* and the *Long Island Star*. We glimpse him working in 1835 and 1836 in New York printing offices and beginning that inveterate play- and opera-going which became for him almost a career in itself in the years before the Civil War. Like many other American writers, beginning with Franklin, Whitman had left school early and embarked on a process of self-education, learning haphazard but useful lessons from the newspaper office, from the general life of the city, and from desultory reading.

In 1836 Walt left the city and returned to rural Long Island, where he was for a year or two a school teacher. One does not wish to burden so ordinary an occurrence with undue significance, especially since it seems to have been largely an inability to support himself in New York that drove him back to the country. Nevertheless, this was the first of those periodic withdrawals from the more highly ordered and businesslike part of the world which are noticeable throughout Whitman's life. He seems to have made one of these strategic withdrawals in the two or three years just before 1855 in preparation for the writing of "Song of Myself" and the other poems of the first edition. He made a recuperative retirement to rural Long Island in the fall of 1855 to absorb and master the disappointment of the failure of his book—he emerged from this withdrawal with the renewed determination (as he declared in the open letter to Emerson which he included in his 1856 edition of *Leaves of Grass*) to dedicate his life to poetry.

There was certainly a powerful reactionary drive in Whitman's personality, a drive too positive to be the result of mere indolence, though of that he had aplenty. One of the characteristic acts of his life is this turning back upon himself, followed by a new advance. It may be said that all living things, and especially all creative human beings, pass through this rhythm. But in Whitman we notice a remarkable preponderance of the reactionary impulse. He seems more often than not to have been passive, psychically slothful, and attached, in a mood of mystery and reverence, to the beginnings, the primitive conditions of his life. Beneath both the frolicksomeness and prophetic egotism of his poetic sensibility there is in Whitman an almost Proustian receptivity and capacity for retrogressive brooding.

In his own way Whitman was conscious of the heavy recalcitrancy and inertia of his being, as is suggested by some of his remarks in later life—such as, "I am a slow arriver: I get there but I always come in last" or "I am the most conservative of conservatives," a phrase to which he gave personal and psychic meanings rather than strictly political ones.

Between 1838 and 1841 Walt was working on newspapers and teaching school. For some months he was on the staff of the *Long Island Democrat*. But his most ambitious project was the *Long Islander*, a paper which he printed himself in Huntington. At this time (1838-9) he even bought a horse on which every week he delivered the paper through the countryside; this occasioned, as he said, many happy "jaunts." It seems also to have occasioned an early bankruptcy, doubtless one of the reverses which led him to remark in later years that "the time of my boyhood was a very restless and unhappy one; I did not know what to do." An account of Walt's habits in about 1840 comes from his landlady, Mrs. Brenton, the wife of the publisher of the *Democrat*. With obvious asperity she describes him as having been slovenly, morose, and withdrawn. He disliked the children in the family; people tripped over his feet as he lolled in a chair; and, Mrs. Brenton complained, he mused and loafed under the blossoming apple trees all afternoon instead of going to the newspaper office. Yet he cannot have been wholly indolent. Considerable prose and verse remain from this period, and by 1840 he had become active in politics, campaigning locally for Van Buren and even making a speech, in July, 1841, at a mass meeting organized in New York by the Tammany Society.

In the *Democrat* Whitman published a series of sketches called "Sun-Down Papers From the Desk of a Schoolmaster." The artificial style he affected and the sentiments he espoused may be seen in paper number five, in which he inculcates temperance: "Amidst the universal excitement which appears to have been created of late years, with regard to the evils created by ardent spirits, it seems to have been forgotten that there are other, and almost as injurious, kinds of intemperance." He proceeds in a tone both facetious and serious to warn of the consequences of too much tea and coffee. Another sketch consists of reflections on death and remarks that when the "Pale Mower" slays an old or middle-aged person, one's grief is "coarse" and has few "refined associations." But what poetic sentiments may not be generated "when we see an infant laid away to a quiet slumber in the bosom of the great mother of men"? In other sketches he resolves to write a great book on the moral dangers of wealth; contrives an elaborate allegory demonstrating that Truth is to be seen only by the naïve; celebrates the "philosophick quietude" induced by loafing; idealizes a kind of tender and healthy but diffuse and disembodied love as against "the puerile, moping love, painted by such trashy writers as Byron and Bulwer." The "Sun-Down Papers" faithfully reflect the popular culture of the time. And, even though they were written as journeywork, they faithfully reflect, also, certain enduring qualities in the author—his abstemiousness, for example, and his preoccupation with death, his plain democratic dislike of wealth, his desire to loaf and invite his soul, his inclination toward a diffuse and nonsexual love.

There was a good deal of dull romanticism in the Whitman of these years of withdrawal. Yet beneath the surface of the pining, restless, and unhappy young man new energies were noticeably stirring. In 1841 he went back to New York and was soon embarked upon a period of relatively busy editing, writing, and politicking. And what is most striking of all, the indolent, overgrown youth who lolled in his chair or under the apple trees became a dandy with a frock coat, a tall hat, a cane, a flower in his lapel, and a carefully nurtured and trimmed beard. A fellow editor on *The Daily Aurora* later recalled that at twenty-two Walt looked twenty-five, was tall, graceful, and neat, and presented "a very pleasing and impressive eye and a cheerful, happy-looking countenance." Despite the brisk appearance, however, Whitman seems actually to have been, even in this relatively energetic period, a somewhat desultory editor. He is said to have made it his custom to reach the *Aurora* office late in the morning, scan the daily papers, and then stroll down Broadway to the Battery, "spending an hour or two amid the trees and enjoying the water view, returning to the office . . . at about 2 or 3 o'clock." Whitman briefly held jobs on several journals in New York and contributed to several others, among them *The Democratic Review*, whose contributors included Hawthorne, Bryant, Thoreau, Whittier, and Poe. Whitman's prose at this time became more literary in its derivations: "Bervance: Or, Father and Son," for example, is a Poesque psychic melodrama about a father who commits his son to a madhouse, though the son is not mad; "A Legend of Life and Love" is a moral allegory in the manner of Hawthorne. One of the first productions of Whitman as a literary critic is a piece called "Boz and Democracy," published in 1842 in *Brother Jonathan*; this is a defense of Dickens against the charge that he is too realistic and writes too much of evil and degradation; Whitman asserts that Dickens is "wholesome" and "a true democratic writer." The influence of Dickens is dimly to be seen in Whitman's most ambitious effort at prose fiction, his temperance tract of 1842 called *Franklin Evans; or the Inebriate*. This short novel is an outrageous piece of vulgarity and was written as hack work by an author who had already lost some of his earlier prudery but not, we may think, his solidly entrenched personal abstemiousness. Whitman said in 1888 of *Franklin Evans*, "It was damned rot . . . not insincere, perhaps, but rot." He liked to say that he had written it in three days "with the help of a bottle of port or what not." Perhaps there was a bottle of port (or as someone else remembered, a series of gin cocktails), but the visions of the drunken newspaperman writing a hack work on temperance which Whitman's words evoke is certainly as mythical as many of the other images by which this romancer and poseur represented himself. The book was truly "rot," however, as the following example of narrative style will suggest:

> There were four of us. The leader of the gang, who was addressed as Picaroon, had several weapons about his person that were evidently capable of doing dangerous work.
>
> "Come, lads," said he, "the business we are on will be none the worse for a few glasses. Let us drink."
>
> At the word, we helped ourselves, and tossed the liquor down our throats.

Such passages as this, together with others of sententious moralizing, are more entertaining than the implausible story of the innocent young hero's narrow escape from the sink of iniquity.

The foppish Walt soon began to give way to the more simply clad but still elegant man of affairs with his copious beard and wide-brimmed hat who turned up, in 1846, as the editor of the Brooklyn *Eagle*. Salutary changes were taking place, in the early 1840's, in Whitman's personality. These were mirrored to some extent in his writing, which begins to show a new capacity to emerge from the smothering fantasies of the unhappy adolescent into an air which, if not exactly open, is nevertheless capable of sustaining a further range of life. The tautness of the dandy, like the grip which prudery and fear of experience had upon the young man, begin to relax. And it is in this period that one of Whitman's most famous characteristics begins fully to manifest itself: his capacity, that is, for absorbing experience, for observing and reporting the mere myriad sights and sounds of things. In these years his "passion for ferries" flowered, as well as his love of "omnibus jaunts and drivers" and "plays and operas too." Such impressions as those of Broadway, which he recorded in *Specimen Days*, helped to put Whitman more widely and deeply in touch with life, helped to furnish out the moral abstractions and fantasies of his mind with concrete meanings or to banish them altogether.

Whitman was editor of the Brooklyn *Eagle* from March, 1846, to January, 1848. The *Eagle* was a flourishing paper which purveyed the attitudes of the Democratic party to the rapidly growing city. Whitman soon became a civic figure as well as a well-known editor. He attended meetings, marched in parades, was made a member of the Fourth of July Celebration Committee, and served as a political functionary. As editor and citizen he attended church services, Sunday school picnics, plays, art exhibits, and concerts. In after years Whitman remembered his job on the *Eagle* as one of the easiest and most pleasant "sits" he had ever had. And indeed, though he probably did more work than he liked to remember, his daily schedule does not sound onerous. He wrote his editorials in the morning, left the office for a walk or lunch, and returned in the afternoon to read proof. Later in the afternoon he habitually went to Gray's Swimming Bath; a former printer's devil remembered years afterward that it had been his custom to accompany Walt to the bath and to pump the water for the editor's shower. The editor often completed his day with a ferry trip to New York, a ride on the horsecars, or a visit to an opera or play.

Whitman's editorials for the *Eagle* are not distinguished; usually they seem desultory or impromptu. That the same is true of his writings for the Brooklyn *Times* (1857-9) proves the inadvisability of taking the *Eagle* editorials as evidence in any account of the development of Whitman's genius. There are certain superficial relationships of theme and attitude between the editorials and the poetry, but far more striking is the almost total impossibility of predicting the poetry, in any exact literary sense, from the editorials. A few of the editorials are interesting, however, as bearing on the poet's life and opinions. His political ideas were Democratic verging later upon the Free Soil position. But I wish to refer here to only two aspects of the *Eagle* editorials: their strain of sentimentality and their view of European literature.

Perhaps Whitman's most amusing editorials are those in which he praises the domestic virtues. How fortunate is that home, he says, where one finds "real quiet enjoyment—the true coy comfort, that loves to nestle in quiet." And how praiseworthy are the novels of Frederika Bremer, wherein we are taught "the mild virtues—how charity and forebearance and love are potent in the domestic circle . . . how indulgence in stormy passions leads invariably to sorrow—and depicting in especial the character of *a good, gentle mother.*" "If we ever have children," concludes the editorialist, "they will read, first, the New Testament, and second, Miss Bremer." This sentimental piety is not, one would gather, mere pretense. Although living at this time with his father and mother, Whitman was already embarked on his semi-Bohemian bachelor's career. But the feeling he exhibits in praising domesticity is one of the many indications that in his sentiments and, indeed, in his profoundest emotional disposition Whitman was conservative and nostalgic.

Whitman's literary nationalism was already established in his mind in the *Eagle* days. He attacks "servile imitation" and plumps for a genuine native literature. One must of course honor "the sweetness and majesty of Shakespeare, Goethe, and some of the Italian poets—the fiery breath of Byron, the fascinating melancholy of Rousseau, the elegance and candor of Hume and Gibbon." Yet the literature of Europe is incurably Tory, or, as he was to say in his later writings, "feudal." Whitman had always loved Scott, especially *The Heart of Midlothian* and the poetry. Yet the American reader must admit that Scott and Southey "exercise an evil influence" through their Toryism. And who must not deplore the "tinsel sentimentality of Bulwer," "the vulgar coarseness of Marryat," "the dishwater senility of Lady Blessington," and "the nastiness of the French Paul De Kock"? "Shall Hawthorne," asks our rhetorician, "shiver with neglect while the public run after this foreign trash?"

We would gather from these editorials that fundamentally Whitman had two objections to European literature: it was undemocratic and it was heterosexual; it spoke of the world as if human beings were divided into classes and the sexes into male and female, and these divisions Whitman could not contemplate without feeling that they were in some way unworthy. His own literary prophetic vision of ideal democracy provides for a world in which these "feudal" distinctions shall, in so far as may prove possible, disappear. The roots of his feeling about the literary treatment of sex are not to be found merely in his democratic credo of equality. They are, of course, neurotic, as will be seen from the fact that when he objects to "sentimentality" in literature, as in speaking of Bulwer, he is always speaking of erotic, heterosexual emotions; he is not objecting to sentimentality as such but to sexuality as such, or at least to the representation of sexuality in literature when this representation is given even the slightest erotic color. This is not at odds with Whitman's poems about sex, such as *Children of Adam* and the *Calamus* poems, which, as has often been observed, do not speak of heterosexuality except in the most remote and abstract language.

The problem of Whitman's sexuality has been closely connected by most biographers with the "New Orleans episode." Whitman was in New Orleans, working on a newspaper called the *Crescent*, from February to May of 1848. With the possible exception of one or two later trips to the South, this was the only extensive journey Whitman made before he published *Leaves of Grass* (he returned from New Orleans, however, by way of the Mississippi, the Great Lakes, Niagara, and the Hudson).

Enticed by the combination of deliberate suppression of fact and the carefully nurtured air of mystery with which Whitman always spoke of his New Orleans venture, some biographers have wanted to see in it the critical moment of his career, although one might more properly believe that for a man of Whitman's organic constitution there can hardly be any one experience upon which his whole life may be said to turn. Whitman was not a man to go from critical experience to critical experience. Rather his life might be called an evasion according to plan. He evaded everything he could, from the pursuits of the workaday world to those isolated religious, imaginative, or sexual experiences which become critical episodes in the lives of other poets. As Whitman himself instinctively knew, his poetic genius would not be liberated by a startling experience, by a ravishing dream, by a vision of God, or by love for a woman or man. It would be self-liberated like leaves of grass, slowly, painfully, and in due time after its long dormancy.

Holloway's *Whitman, An Interpretation in Narrative* was one of the semipopular "Freudian" biographies of the 1920's, and the emphasis it makes on the New Orleans episode may be taken as typical of a whole school of biographers (although, as one may think, a genuinely Freudian view of Whitman's life might lead to conclusions different from Holloway's). There being no indisputable evidence that Walt Whitman became involved with one or more women in New Orleans, the biographers have had to content themselves with putting together scraps of dubious evidence. Most arresting of these is Whitman's letter to John Addington Symonds, written at Camden in 1890, wherein the poet's would-be disciple was told:

My life, young manhood, mid-age, times South, etc., have been jolly bodily, and doubtless open to criticism. Though unmarried I have had six children—two are dead—one living Southern grandchild, fine boy, writes to me occasionally—circumstances (connected with their fortune and benefit) have separated me from intimate relations.

Although the burden of proof would seem to be on Whitman or on his six children, one cannot say with absolute certainty that his statement is pure fabrication. Yet on the whole the presumption is that the "six children" were invented by an old man who wished to call off the dogs of a young idealist bent on securing from him an admission that the *Calamus* poems might be taken as the Bible of homosexual love. One may guess that Whitman, weak and tired in 1890, may have taken what he thought to be the quickest way to scotch the rather involved and Platonized homosexual idealism of writers like Symonds, in so far as they tried to derive it from *Leaves of Grass*. Clearly the imputation worried, confused, and annoyed him.

The other scraps of "evidence" for the New Orleans sexual experience are much less striking than the letter to Symonds. There is, for example, the sketch called "A Night at the Terpsichore Ball" published in the *Crescent* (a story telling how the author got himself introduced to a beautiful and cultivated lady by a man who later turns out to be her husband —but this sounds like standard popular humor, not autobiography). There is another piece in the *Crescent* defending nude statuary. (What a momentous loss to civilization that Whitman and Hawthorne did not engage in a dialogue on this matter!) There is Whitman's knowledgeable description of the New Orleans octoroons—"women with splendid bodies, no bustles, no corsets, no enormities of any sort; large luminous bright eyes; face a rich olive; habits indolent, yet not

lazy as we define laziness North; always more than pretty—
'pretty' is too weak a word to apply to them." The poem
"Once I Pass'd Through a Populous City," which contains the
line "Yet now of all that city I remember only a woman I cas-
ually met there who detain'd me for love of me," was often
cited as referring to New Orleans and lending credibility to
Whitman's connection with a woman, until it was discovered
that in another, earlier version of the poem the poet spoke of
himself as being detained not by a "woman" but a "man."

The arguments for "the New Orleans woman" have often
taken a purely literary turn. Holloway, for example, saw in
Whitman's visit to New Orleans a pilgrimage of the naïve
Northerner to the Paris of the South. In New Orleans "Whitman had found himself akin, through the flesh, with all mankind;" and this broadening of experience had a liberating
effect so that, as Holloway suggested, "the floodgates of a
highly sexed nature, the 'pent-up rivers' of himself gave way,
and Whitman returned to nature" (as we worldlings of the
fifties return to the vivid biographers of the twenties). Behind the scenes of this drama of self-transcendence there lurks
a shadowy octoroon, to be compared with Shakespeare's Dark
Lady and Melville's Fayaway.

It is difficult to think of Whitman as having "a highly sexed
nature." We are not bound, either, to believe that even if he
did have a woman or women in New Orleans or elsewhere,
this would have been a critical event in his life. If in some
sense the hypothetical experience might be regarded as crucial, there is good reason for thinking that it gave Whitman,
or confirmed in him, a basic feeling of remoteness from
women, rather than leading him to a new connection with life
and nature.

The facts known at present about Whitman seem to accord
with a very indifferently, rather than a highly, sexed nature.
There is considerable evidence to show that he may have

made connections with both sexes, although none of it is conclusive. He seemed in person oddly bisexual, his body being
large and sturdy but without any apparent musculature beneath the soft feminine flesh. There seems no doubt that he
had inclinations in both directions—whether or not there ever
was a "Washington woman" or New Orleans octoroon or a
series of young stage drivers or Civil War veterans like his
friend Pete Doyle. We find a number of cryptic jottings in his
notebooks of 1868-70, for example, which suggest a confused
and hectic sexual versatility. *"Pursue her no more,"* he ad-
monishes himself (this passage does not seem to be mere
phrenological jargon, as has been maintained). Again he
writes, "Depress the adhesive nature. . . . It is in excess—
making life a torment." This *is* phrenological jargon, "adhesive" referring to the comradely love of males. That he had
at times a homosexual sensibility is shown by a letter he wrote
to some of his New York companions during the Washington
days:

> Only I have some curious yarns I promise you my
> darlings & gossips, by word of mouth whene're we
> meet. . . .
>
> I remain yet much of the old vagabond that so
> gracefully becomes me. I miss you my darlings & gos-
> sips, Fred Gray, & Bloom and Russell and every-
> body. . . .
>
> My health, strength, personal beauty, etc., are, I am
> happy to inform you, without diminution, but on the
> contrary quite the reverse. I weigh full 220 pounds
> avoirdupois. Yet still retain my usual perfect shape—a
> regular model.

Perhaps the best supposition about Whitman is that he was
sexually versatile, that he was more strongly drawn to men
than to women, but that probably his life was not overtly and
actually sexual at all, since he always found ways of converting

his sexual impulses to artistic ends or generalizing them into a vague, diffuse, and psychically infantile feeling of "comradeship."

To conclude the New Orleans episode, it would be wrong to discount altogether its influence on Whitman's development. It must indeed have had some strong effect on a young man who had already manifested an extraordinary capacity for absorbing experience, for taking in the sights and sounds of the world with a unique sense of wonder and freshness. There were experiences to be had in New Orleans in 1848, besides that of making a mistress of an octoroon. Unfortunately we do not know much of what Walt did in New Orleans —*Specimen Days,* in which he records at least something of what was memorable in his life, mentions his days on the *Crescent* only in passing. But we do know (from his newspaper articles) that he had seen new vistas, observed new types, exposed his omnivorous sensibility to a new part of the world, seen depths of degradation and manifestations of colorful temperament unknown in Brooklyn. In the language of "Song of Myself" it was a new advance in "identification," in drawing into the self the experience of the world.

There is little to record of the years between 1848 and 1855. Whitman's career as a journalist at this time seems even more inconsequential and subject to misfortune than in previous years; and one has the sense, if only from the dearth of information, that the really meaningful and exciting events of Whitman's life were now interior, where the hesitant but restless "embryons" of *Leaves of Grass* were stirring. The most auspicious outward event was his becoming editor, soon after his return from New Orleans, of a new paper in Brooklyn called the *Freeman*. He was appropriately hailed by a rival paper which announced that "Rienzi has returned . . . our old Barnburner friend himself." As the name indicates, the editorial policy of the new paper was to be Free Soil. But the plant where the *Freeman* was printed burned down on the night of the first issue, and although Whitman was able to resume publication after two months, the times were not propitious for the venture, the Free Soil party being, for one thing, on its way to rejoining the regular Democratic party. After a year Whitman left the paper, with an editorial assurance that he was grateful to his friends and associates, and concluding: "My enemies—and old Hunkers generally—I disdain and defy the same as ever.—Walter Whitman." Between 1849 and 1851 Whitman, besides doing free-lance writing and perhaps compositing, maintained an unsuccessful printing office and store in a building whose second floor was inhabited for a time by his father's family. The memory of Walt's brother George was that in these years Walt had not worked regularly, that he rose late, did a lot of reading, and wrote a great deal, mostly lectures as the family thought, though, as George said, "we did not know what he was writing." Even less eventful were the years between 1851 and 1854. It was then that Walt took to carpentering with his father and achieved his final transformation, as Perry remarked, from the young dandy to the "quiet, slow-footed, grey-bearded working man." One has occasional glimpses of activities later to be productive of poetry—Whitman's habit of reading Emerson's essays during the lunch hour, for instance, and his reading of Homer, Sophocles, Shakespeare, the Bible, and Epictetus (a lifelong favorite). He seems also to have spent a part of every summer wandering about rural Long Island, whose country influences he always found so profoundly restful and recruiting, as well as instinct with moral and poetic qualities.

Whitman was one of those writers who, like Mark Twain, Shaw, Dostoevsky, and Yeats, present themselves through their art or their public life in the guise of more than one self. (In his notebook Whitman had written, perhaps as early as

1847, "I cannot understand the mystery, but I am always conscious of myself as two." And he provisionally identified the "two" as "my soul and I.") Invoking the Dionysian rites and the Aristophanic comedy, Nietzsche asserted the necessity of the double personality. "Everything that is profound loves the mask," he wrote; "the profoundest things have a hatred even of figure and likeness. Should not the *contrary* be the right disguise for the shame of a God to go about in?" Like other modern writers Whitman found it temperamentally pleasurable as well as strategically necessary to interpose a half-ironic image of himself between the world and that profound part of his personality which hated figure and likeness—the unconscious mind with its spontaneous, lawless, poetic impulses. He invented not one but several public personalities—the worldly, dandified young metropolitan journalist of the early 1840's; the homely, Christlike carpenter and radical of the early 1850's; the full-bearded, sunburned, clean-limbed, vigorously sexed, burly common man of the later fifties and early sixties; the male nurse and good gray poet of the Washington period; the sage of Camden of the late years.

In having contrived so striking a procession of public images (actually all but the young journalist-dandy are aspects of one large public gesture) Whitman is unique among American writers. The masks interest us only because we see that they are not assumed merely to fool the public. There was, to be sure, a certain strain of insincerity in Whitman. He wrote anonymous panegyrics of *Leaves of Grass* and generally puffed his own writings when he got the chance. He allowed early biographies of himself to be published (he even collaborated more or less in their composition) which contained misleading information, such as, that the author of *Leaves of Grass* had, by 1855, traveled throughout the United States and therefore knew at first hand the geographical phenomena the poems celebrate. Yet without wishing to condone dishonesty, one may suggest that modern Americans are far too sensitive about sincerity—except in personal relationships, it is after all one of the minor virtues. Whitman may have gone off the deep end in pursuit of sympathy and comradeship, but at least he does not come bounding up to us with that doglike guilelessness our contemporary culture admires. He wore the mask of the American humorist; he was quirky, ironic, "indirect," guileful. As he remarked to Edward Carpenter, one of his English admirers, "There is something in my nature *furtive* like an old hen! . . . Sloane Kennedy [another disciple] calls me 'artful'—which about hits the mark."

Whitman was a democratic version of that modern personality adumbrated in the *Rameau's Nephew* of Diderot—the divided, multiple personality, a shifting amalgam of sycophancy and sloth, of mimetic brilliance and Dionysian inspiration, of calculating common sense and philosophic insight, of raffish Bohemianism, of Rousseauistic disorientation and primitivism—a mind neurotic, lonely, unstable, libidinous, envious, indolent, suffused with yeasty eruptions from the unconscious depths, turning uncertainly from self-assertion to self-recrimination and despair, brooding with the same sense of mystery on the most sublime and the most vulgar and sordid aspects of life.

As I say, one is not for long touched or interested by a writer's public poses when these are too preponderantly fake —as in the case of Oscar Wilde. The poses, we feel, must be largely a necessity induced in the writer by his own personality or by the culture he lives in. Certainly they were so induced in Whitman.

Looked at as a matter of public relations, the problem is simple. Whitman was a poet of a very advanced and difficult sort; he was of dubious sex. This gave him two wars to fight with the advancing bourgeois America, and two wars to fight with himself, so much a part was he of this America, so much did he share in its tastes and believe in its moral proscriptions. The culture of his time admired (much more so than our culture does today) the prophet, the orator, the sententious democratic reformer; and it admired rough plebeian masculinity. It would condone oddity of behavior (more so than now) so long as the main requirements were met. Whitman met them. When he discovered how strong was the public condemnation of sex in literature, Whitman added to the façade the "good gray poet" (or gratefully allowed it to be added by his disciple and apologist O'Connor). These poses are, of course, involved extensively in Whitman's poetry, a large portion of *Leaves of Grass* being little more than a rhetorical proclamation of them. From the point of view of art and under the aspect of eternity the public figure and his democratic program (valuable as these are in themselves) were the massive irrelevance and waste required for the indulgence of the essential Whitman—the young comic god and profound elegist.

Whitman had it somewhat easier than Melville or Mark Twain. Neurotic, riven, and vividly paradoxical as his personality was, many of the conflicting elements were subsumable under his monumental inertia and placidity, which allowed him to live more at rest than they in nineteenth-century America. The battle of Melville and Mark Twain with their times, though not more fundamental than that of Whitman, was more violent and more wearing. One might find a genetic explanation for this in the fact that all three had rather unstable fathers who "failed," but that whereas Melville and Mark Twain had mothers who were inclined to be harsh and morally overbearing and for whom they came to have very equivocal feelings, Whitman's mother was what is supposed to be the American male's ideal—she was firm, patient, hard-working, sympathetic and loving, and she lived on in her son.

In effect Whitman was cannier than either Melville or Mark Twain. His battle was more covert, more furtive; his essential genius was buried deep in his massive, slow-moving personality, showed itself on few occasions (not at all until he was thirty-six), masked itself behind a consistent and extensive series of public gestures, and quickly disappeared altogether. Despite the failure of *Leaves of Grass*, Whitman did not suffer the long nervous exacerbations of Melville and Mark Twain. One may note that Van Wyck Brooks was wrong to suggest, in *The Ordeal of Mark Twain*, that when Whitman retired to Camden in 1873, he was retreating like a whipped dog from a hostile and unappreciative America—this is the kind of speculation that invites the philistine reply: "No, he went because he had a stroke and his brother George lived in Camden." (I would add, however, that after critics like Bernard De Voto have recaptured nineteenth-century American culture in what plenitude it had, Brooks' biography of Mark Twain seems still *essentially* right, although errant in many particulars. His book remains a classic in the study of the position of our great writers in the nineteenth century.)

Is Whitman, then, an example of what is known as the alienated artist? Certainly there is much evidence to convince us that he gave people the impression of living outside the usual order of things, related to but different from the world of ordinary men—an impression which encouraged his disciples in later years to regard him as a genuinely new species of man and to approach him with something of that awe which mankind reserves for the shaman, the holy idiot, prophet, or priest. This peculiar estrangement from the world is one of the striking facts about Whitman. One notices that, for reasons among which his bisexuality must figure prominently, he never had any relationships with others which were not strongly susceptible of abstract and ideal meaning; the give and take of ordinary human friendship were unknown to him.

His relationships were those of the loving son to the blameless mother, the tender father to the idealized young man (the wounded veteran, the young horsecar driver), the master to his disciples. Especially in his later years people found Whitman cold, secretive, stubbornly impersonal but at the same time paradoxically wistful and appealing.

This alienation, impelling Whitman to resort to symbolic and ideal forms of reattachment, is one of the major sources of his art. And one may think that he was a great poet as long as he could believe in the availability, reality, and endurance of the self that gazed in wonder at the world and as long as he could accept its apartness either by proclamations of the power of the self alone or of the identity of the self with all things and all men. Thus in "Song of Myself" (to anticipate for a moment) the world and its people are seen from a position apart: "they are not the Me myself." But the separation is nothing to fear, because however illusory the world may be, nothing can alienate the self: "What is commonest, cheapest, nearest, easiest is Me." The decline of Whitman the great poet begins when he comes to think that he is alienated not only from the world but from himself and that this alienation can no longer be felt as a challenge to be met by aggressive poetic expression or in contemplative elegiac verse but is felt, rather, as a threat which can be met only by extra-poetic means—by becoming, that is, the hospital visitor, the self-publicist, the good gray poet, the sage and master. The perception of this self-alienation, the sense of "the real Me" being "withdrawn far, mocking me," is expressed in the beautiful elegy "As I Ebb'd with the Ocean of Life."

If the masks he wore and the poems he wrote served Whitman as façades to hide behind, they also served to symbolize and countervail or deny his alienation. As Mark Van Doren says, "Whitman's best poetry came out of his contradictions, and out of his struggle either to resolve them or to remove them." Van Doren adds that Whitman was far from the average man he talked of being; indeed, a gulf opens "between him and us, and leaves him standing strangely on the other side. Across such a space we can contemplate better than we formerly could his predilection for the theme of death." When the gulf across which Whitman stared at the rest of the world and finally at himself could no longer be symbolically bridged, it became in itself the obsessive object of contemplation.

Sociologically speaking, Whitman's poses were the reflex of his culture. From the point of view of his art, they were the concerted maneuver which allowed him to produce a small body of great poetry. Psychologically speaking, they were the ego ideals which sought to control an unruly unconscious, or to mediate between it and the world. If we turn to the difficult, and doubtless insoluble, problem of explaining how, apparently almost overnight, Walt Whitman ceased being merely a desultory editor, hack writer and carpenter and became a great poet, we will doubtless conclude that only a line of psychological speculation can avoid sententious irrelevancies. Of course, it will not solve the problem. (There is hardly any literary evidence which allows us to trace a development of either thought or style. The scanty notebooks, going back as early as 1847, are of little interest. The few scattered examples of Whitman's early poetry, extending from imitations of Scott to a broken versification dimly resembling that of *Leaves of Grass*, are of some technical interest. They raise the question—but hardly more—as to how Whitman achieved the language without which he would not have been a poet. In this connection, however, the reader may find the concluding pages of chapter II of interest.)

The three most frequently recurring explanations of Whitman's transformation from editor-carpenter to poet seem inadmissible. The first is that New Orleans and the octoroon

Whitman met there converted the provincial Quakerish youth to life and liberated his creative powers. If we are right in thinking that Whitman was rather virginal than overtly sexual, we cannot give credence to the New Orleans explanation, in so far as this refers to a sexual connection. And in any case even so slow a personality as Whitman's would probably not require seven years (from 1848-1855) to exhibit the results of so momentous an experience.

A second explanation is that at some time after the New Orleans trip and subsequent adventures probably involving sexual attempts, Whitman had the tragic but purgative and liberating experience of recognizing and accepting the fact that he was homosexual. But here again the objection must be that Whitman's sexuality was so diffuse and sublimated that it could never have generated in him any definitive disposition or crucial recognition and acceptance of such a disposition. Furthermore, the evidence that Whitman had heterosexual relations is almost as substantial as the evidence that he was homosexual—and neither is *very* substantial.

A third explanation is that Whitman had a mystical experience, not necessarily involving sex, which gave him his characteristic vision, that at some crucial moment he was "illuminated" and perceived the universe in all its totality—"cosmic consciousness," Dr. Richard Bucke, one of the disciples and an "alienist," called it. Observers so acute as Santayana and William James concluded that the essential quality of Whitman's mind was mysticism, although to the literary critic it does not seem so. Comparisons have been made between Whitman and the Oriental mystics; St. Paul and Rousseau, struck down by the apocalyptic influx of light, have been recalled. There may be sometimes a kind of mysticism at work in Whitman's poetry. But it is hardly ever distinguishable from merely vague thought and diffuse metaphor—and therefore it seems more gratuitous or honorific than accurate to refer to it as mysticism. But from a literary point of view this "mysticism" is surely not "characteristic." And in fact the more one reviews the evidence and the more one reads the poems, the less likely does the "mystical experience" seem and the less relevant to an understanding of such poems as "Song of Myself" does it become, even if it occurred. As we have noted before, there is no evidence about Whitman which encourages us to think him capable of any stern, overwhelming, or intense spiritual experience. Except in his poems, his mind and emotions were not grasping, imperious and rapid like those of St. Paul or Rousseau, nor capable of the disciplined masochism of the Oriental mystic. Whitman made the right analogy: he was like the grass, he was a "slow arriver," his poetic powers emerged gradually and painfully, and whatever definitive redispositions there were were secret and subliminal but of the native soil.

Furthermore, it seems a matter of general principle that poetic experience, although it may include it, cannot be equated with or produced by mystic experience, properly so called. Mysticism leads to the ecstatic contemplation of the naught; it does not of itself produce poetry, which is a metaphorical construction of the aught. Poetry is made by the imagination, and, as Santayana insists, the life of reason depends on our ability to distinguish between the imaginative and the mystic (although he himself failed to do so in his attack on Whitman). I do not wish to deny the usefulness of the word "mysticism" in speaking of the general tenor of Whitman's mind, but only to doubt its relevance to the strictly literary question and to the question of his emergence as a poet.

A more convincing line of speculation as to how Whitman became a poet probably has to begin with the theory developed by Jean Catel in his *Walt Whitman: la naissance du poète* (1929), a much more solid piece of Freudian analysis than Holloway's. Catel notes the morose, disorganized per-

sonality of Walt's father, the anxious instability of the family
as it moved from house to house, the unfolding fate of Walt's
brothers and sisters which, as we have noted, was to be on the
whole a story of sickness, depravity, and insanity—when Alcott visited Whitman in 1856 he found that Walt shared a bed
with his twenty-one-year-old brother Eddie, the imbecile and
epileptic. One observes the uncertainty of Whitman's life as
a young man, after he had emerged from what the poet himself called his "unhappy" boyhood. From the time Walt began to work in printing shops up until 1855, and thereafter
for that matter, his career consisted of a series of advances
and retreats, of abortive attempts to hold jobs, to become a
writer of editorials, sketches and short stories. One postulates
the failure and pain of the young man's sexual experiments,
the anxiety consequent upon his gradual realization of his
bisexuality and his auto-eroticism—the "I" in "Song of Myself" has two aspects or voices: the wistful, lonely, hurt, feminine, erotically demanding voice which alternates with that
of the bearded, sunburned, masculine, democratic "rough."
And the poem contains passages, of course, which are frankly
auto-erotic.

The emergence of Whitman's genius may be understood as
the consequence of his having failed because of neurotic dis-
turbances to make terms with the world. In the early 1850's
he found a compensatory way of dealing with a world which
threatened to defeat him. If he could not subdue it on its own
terms, he would do so by committing himself entirely to that
rich fantasy life of which he felt himself increasingly capable.
(That Whitman conceived of his own poetic emergence in a
way that substantiates the present argument is shown by his remark that "the *Democratic Review* essays and tales came
from the surface of the mind, and had no connection with
what lay below—a great deal of which indeed was below consciousness. At last came the time when the concealed growth

had to come to light.") His power of fantasy would allow him to escape into an innocent, regressive, Eden-like realm and it would also allow him symbolically to assault and overwhelm a world of ordinary reality which had proved to be, on its own terms, too much for him. He would utterly escape and defy the world's attempt to establish in his shifting psychic economy a superego—to impose upon him this or that conventional "identity." He would allow his unconscious the freedom it demanded. He would free the ego of all prudential considerations, and make it dance to the tune of the unconscious. He would write a poem full of the sense of release and novelty, redolent with the uncanny unpredictableness of images fresh from the subliminal mind, and the subject of the poem would be the self—that is, the unconscious mind—"the infinite and omnigenous" self, and it would describe the self as a timeless universal continuum but also as having the capacity to advance and retreat, to merge with and to extricate itself at will from any and all "identities." The poem would be full of philosophy and high thought, to be sure, but it would purvey the philosophy in a style determined by the sheer solipsism and incongruity of unconscious thought.

So free and aggressive an assertion of unconscious impulse, like any outburst that flouts the prudent, moralizing part of the mind, might be expected to generate a good deal of guilt. And this will account in part for the rather extensive revisions Whitman made of "Song of Myself" in later editions, carefully excising or rewording sections which spoke too frankly of such matters as adolescent sexual confusions. It will account for his deliberate silence about what he was doing in the period just before 1855, and it gives us a lead toward explaining the whole elaborate evasion which constituted his public pose and which he fostered and condoned in the early biographies. Whitman was by no means always the free spirit he was in "Song of Myself." Taking him by and large, he was

canny and prudential. In an early notebook he had written
that to be an American "is to be illimitably proud, independent, self-possessed, generous, and gentle. It is to accept nothing except what is equally free and eligible to anybody else.
It is to be poor rather than rich—but to prefer death sooner
than any mean dependence. . . . Prudence is part of it, because prudence is the right arm of independence." Nothing
could be more characteristic of Whitman than that last sentence. It reminds one of his amusing exhortation to Traubel
in later years: "Be radical, be radical, be not too damn radical."

The analysis of Whitman's personality set forth in the last
paragraphs cannot, of course, fully account for Whitman the
poet. It is impossible to say why, given his psychic difficulties,
he became a poet and not (like his brother Jesse) a psychotic
case, except that he had "genius." On a historical view, however, one notices a happy conjunction of forces, involving
Whitman's emerging personality and the assumptions of the
culture he lived in, partly as Whitman instinctively understood and shared them, partly as he found them rationalized
and given a language in the essays of Emerson.

In order to arrive at the vision of things which we find in
"Song of Myself," the self had to be apprehended as a felt
presence, as an idea, and as a metaphor or conceit. It had to
be identified with the unconscious at least completely enough
so that it would take on to itself some of the powers and qualities of the unconscious. But first (the chronology is, of course,
for purposes of discussion only) Whitman had to liberate
within himself and become aware of his unconscious mind in
its poetry-making aspect. That he had done this by 1855 is
shown by another poem which appeared in the first edition,
"The Sleepers." As we shall note below, this poem is of interest to the psychological investigator because of its presentation of the dream activity of the mind as the way in which

universal equality and unity are achieved, the way in which joy and vitality are released, and, most important, the way in which the poetic imagination is achieved.

Given the unconscious so conceived, what was needed before "Song of Myself" could be written was the idea of the self and some reason for connecting the self with the unconscious. Several things forced the self upon Whitman's attention. He was characteristically, as he said, conscious of himself as "two" (psychologically perhaps the result of his bisexual nature). The democracy of which Whitman was so natively a part exalted the free, self-sufficient individual, having lost under the impact of Jeffersonian and Jacksonian theories much of whatever sense of traditional, institutional life and the place of the individual therein it had once possessed. The Quaker tendency of the Whitman family enhanced the sense of the inner mystery. Transcendentalist theory made the self a godlike power—omniscient, omnipresent, omnipotent. In "Self-Reliance" Emerson mythicized the self in a way which could hardly fail to have the most conclusive and electric effect on a mind such as Whitman's.

> What is the aboriginal self, on which a universal reliance may be grounded? [Emerson asked.] The inquiry leads us to that source, at once the essence of genius, of virtue, and of life, which we call spontaneity or instinct. We denote this primary wisdom as intuition, whilst all later teachings are tuitions. In that deep force, the last fact behind which analysis cannot go, all things find their common origin.

Taking a psychological view of this characteristic formulation (as the references to "spontaneity," "instinct," and the "deep force" of the mind allow us to do), we understand Emerson to say that an inquiry into the self, both in its individual and its universal aspects, leads us to the unconscious part of the mind. In another sense, Emerson is apparently saying that the self, considered as "aboriginal," *is* the unconscious, that in its aboriginal aspect, it not only leads us to the unconscious —to the "last fact behind which analysis cannot go"—it *is* this "last fact."

One need not find Emerson's words perfectly clear as psychology or metaphysics to see in them a remarkably suggestive and fertile poetic metaphor. And it must certainly have been as such that the formulation appealed to Whitman. In this basic metaphor Emerson can be said to have made connections among the self or identity, the unconscious, and the universal, and to have given the whole vision the status of "wisdom" in just such a manner as would precipitate a similar crystalization in the mind of Whitman. All the elements were in Whitman, the products of his peculiar temperament and of his democratic surroundings. But it was from Emerson that he first sensed how they might be put together.

The release and acceptance of unconscious poetry-making powers is described in "The Sleepers." As the *Whitman Handbook* avers, it has long been recognized that "no other composition is so revealing of the methods by which [Whitman] sublimated his life into the universal symbols of poetry." A detailed reading of the poem would be tedious and probably misleading. But as a way of penetrating the evocative surface of "The Sleepers" the burdensome language of science may prove temporarily useful. "The Sleepers" is a poem about the descent of the as yet unformed and unstable ego into the id, its confrontation there of the dark, human tragedy, its emergence in a new, more stable form. Or in Whitmanesque language, the subject of the poem is the surrender of the self to the "night," the identification of the self with the "night" and the subsequent emergence of the self, newly constituted and participant in forms of unity, health, and felicity. At the beginning, the poet is "wandering and confused, lost to myself, ill-assorted, contradictory." But at the end—having dared to descend into the night so that now he can defiantly exclaim, "Why should I be afraid to trust myself to you?"—the wandering has direction, the self is no longer alienated, abysses are bridged, contradictions resolved.

To follow Whitman while, as he says, "I become the other dreamers" is to encounter a series of hauntingly beautiful if sometimes elusive emotions and symbols. There is the gratifying sense of surrender and release, impelling the poet to exclaim:

> I am a dance—play up there! The fit is whirling me
> fast!
> I am the ever-laughing. . . .
> Onward we move, a gay gang of blackguards! with
> mirth-shouting music and wild-flapping pennants
> of joy!

There are the more somber moments when we behold the dark motives and characters of that family drama which underlies some of the greatest of tragic poems. Insistently present is the encompassing image of the mother, who appears in the guise of the young woman who receives a shadowy lover, as the "sleepless widow" who looks out on "the winter midnight" and sees the shrouded coffin of her husband, and as the goddess-like squaw whom, like so many things in this poem, Whitman recalls from childhood experience. The mother plays her central part among the shifting scenes in which we catch a glimpse of the "beautiful gigantic swimmer swimming naked through the eddies of the sea" until, bruised on the rocks, he is borne "swiftly and out of sight," [a] "brave corpse"; in which we stand with the poet on a frozen, wintry beach watching while the corpses of a wrecked ship's passengers are brought ashore; and in which we see George Washington, cold, weeping, and pale, bidding farewell, in his tender, fatherly manner, to his surviving soldiers.

The dark actions of the poem having been played out, the conflicts and guilt feelings having been allayed, the ostensibly ill-assorted personages having been brought into relation, there can follow a pleasurable idyl which celebrates forms of unity. "The wildest and bloodiest is over, and all is peace." No longer is the poet "lost" to himself. Alienation, separation, contradiction—these sources of unconscious conflict and pain but also of rationality and imagination are not abolished; rather they are envisioned as parts of a larger order. So Whitman seems to mean when he says that "the diverse shall be no less diverse, but they shall flow and unite—they unite now." The flow and the unity refer no doubt to Whitman's "philosophy," his idea of a dialectically emergent, creative, and benign universe. But they also refer to his unique poetic method, the achievement of which "The Sleepers" may be understood to announce and describe. The self has been powerfully reconstituted by its descent into the night and so is ready to perform its vivid feats in "Song of Myself." But so has the poetic style which a difficult subject demands. Such a complicated and unique style cannot be defined easily, and I wish to do no more at this point than to observe, what other writers have noticed, that a stream-of-consciousness method underlies the structure of Whitman's poetry. He is likely to be at his very best when a cat-and-mouse game is going on between the conscious and the unconscious, when unexpected dreamlike images emerge apparently unheralded and have to be dealt with by an imaginative intelligence which is not often capable of large, executive organizations of meaning but which is triumphantly capable of local forms of order produced by a comic or elegiac sensibility. Of all Whitman's poems "The Sleepers" is nearest to a pure stream-of-consciousness method, with its impressive flow of what seem absolutely inevitable archetypal images. This poem is characteristic of Whitman at his best; for where the self is dancing, penetrating the veil of death, confronting exciting emanations from the unconscious, and rebounding into the midst of life, it is always an interesting protagonist.

The evidence, if such it may be accounted, of "The Sleepers" would seem to suggest anew the improbability that a decisive mystical or sexual experience was what transformed Whitman from a journalist and carpenter into a poet. This poem implies that "the diverse," could now be made to "flow and unite" because the poet had reached the point where he could liberate his inner energies by a return to his earliest memories, long suppressed perhaps but now freed and imaginatively symbolized. This inner psychic advance happily coincided with the effect upon Whitman's imagination of certain cultural and literary influences, the most important of which were suggested above. All this is of course a truism, in the sense that it describes the way in which all poets become poets. But the ingenuous critic will pretend to offer no more, and may rest content with having suggested some of the particular qualities of his particular truism.

CHAPTER II

"ONE'S SELF I SING"

THE MAIN ITEM of the 1855 edition of *Leaves of Grass* was, of course, "Song of Myself," the profound and lovely comic drama of the self which is Whitman's best poem and contains in essence nearly all, yet not quite all, there is to *Leaves of Grass*. The comic spirit of the poem is of the characteristic American sort, providing expression for a realism at once naturalistic and transcendental, for the wit, gaiety, and festive energy of all good comedy, and also for meditative soliloquy, at once intensely personal and strongly generic.

One circumstance that contributes to the general spontaneity of "Song of Myself" is, in fact, Whitman's unsuccessful attempt to be an Emersonian or Wordsworthian moralist. In his preface, he wrote that "of all mankind the poet is the equable man. Not in him but off from him things are grotesque or eccentric or fail of their sanity . . . He is the arbiter of the diverse and he is the key. He is the equalizer of his age and land." Whitman tries, indeed, to install himself in his poem on this high moral ground: he will, he says, first regenerate himself by leaving the fallacious artificialities of modern life and getting back to fundamentals; then, having perfected himself as the norm, he will summon all the world to him to be freed of its abnormalities. But although in the poem the self remains pretty much at the center of things, Whitman finds it impossible to accept the idea that

it is a norm. To the sententious prophet who "promulges"
the normative self, the comic poet and ironic realist keep in-
troducing other, disconcertingly eccentric selves.

> Who goes there? hankering, gross, mystical, nude. . . .

Whoever he is, he is not in a position to utter morality. The
self in this poem *is* (to use Lawrence's phrase) "tricksy-
tricksy"; it does "shy all sorts of ways" and is finally, as the
poet says, "not a bit tamed," for "I too am untranslatable."
So that as in all true, or high, comedy, the sententious, the
too overtly insisted-on morality (if any) plays a losing game
with ironical realism. In the social comedy of Molière, Congreve, or Jane Austen, moral sententiousness, like other de-
formities of comportment or personality, is corrected by
society. But this attitude is, of course, foreign to Whitman,
who has already wished to invite society to correct itself by
comparing itself with him and who, furthermore, cannot
even sustain this democratic inversion of an aristocratic idea.
Whitman's comic poetry deflates pretensions and chides moral
rigidity by opposing to them a diverse, vital, indeterminate
reality.

   "I resist anything better than my own diversity," says Whitman, and this is the characteristic note of "Song of Myself."
Not that by referring to "Song of Myself" as a "comic" poem
I wish too narrowly to limit the scope of discussion—nor do I
suggest in using the term a special theory of Whitman or of
American literature. I simply respond to my sense that "Song
of Myself" is on the whole comic in tone and that although
the poem's comic effects are of universal significance, they
often take the specific form of American humor. If one finds
"Song of Myself" enjoyable at all, it is because one is conscious of how much of the poem, though the feeling in many
of its passages need not perhaps have been comic at all, nevertheless appeals to one, first and last, in its comic aspect. The

poem is full of odd gestures and whimsical acts; it is written by a neo-Ovidian poet for whom self-metamorphosis is almost as free as free association, who can write "I am an old artillerist" or "I will go to the bank by the wood, and become undisguised and naked" as easily as he can write:

> Askers embody themselves in me and I am embodied
>   in them,
> I project my hat, sit shame-faced, and beg.

The sense of incongruous diversity is very strong in "Song of Myself," and although one does not know how the sly beggar projecting his hat or the martial patriot is transformed into the "acme of things accomplish'd," and "encloser of things to be" who suddenly says:

> I find I incorporate gneiss, coal, long-threaded moss,
>   fruits, grains, esculent roots,
> And am stucco'd with quadrupeds and birds all over,

one is nevertheless charmed with the transformation.

Whitman conceives of the self, one might say, as James conceives of Christopher Newman in *The American*—as having the "look of being committed to nothing in particular, of standing in an attitude of general hospitality to the chances of life." In other words, the "self" who is the protagonist of Whitman's poem is a character portrayed in a recognizable American way; it illustrates the fluid, unformed personality exulting alternately in its provisional attempts to define itself and in its sense that it has no definition. The chief difference between "Song of Myself" and *The American* is, of course, the difference between the stages on which Whitman and James allow the self to act, James confining the action to his international scene and Whitman opening his stage out into an eventful universe which is a contradictory but witty collocation of the natural and the transcendent, the imperfect

and the utopian, the personal and the generic—a dialectic
world out of whose "dimness opposite equals advance" and
in which there is "always a knot of identity" but "always distinction."

The very scope of Whitman's universe and the large freedom he assumes to move about in it allowed him to appropriate new areas of experience and thus to make of "Song of
Myself" the original and influential poem it is. For one thing,
this is the first American poem to invade that fruitful ground
between lyric verse and prose fiction that so much of modern
poetry cultivates, and one may suppose that "Song of Myself"
has had at least as much effect on the novel as, let us say,
Moby Dick or *The Golden Bowl* have had on poetry. The famous lines in Section 8 are, at any rate, both "imagistic"
and novelistic:

> The little one sleeps in its cradle;
> I lift the gauze and look a long time, and silently brush
>   away flies with my hand.
> The youngster and the red-faced girl turn aside up the
>   bushy hill;
> I peeringly view them from the top.
> The suicide sprawls on the bloody floor of the bed-
>   room;
> I witness the corpse with its dabbled hair, I note where
>   the pistol has fallen.

It is probably true that more than anyone else, more than
Blake or Baudelaire, Whitman made the city poetically
available to literature:

> The blab of the pave, tires of carts, sluff of boot-soles,
>   talk of the promenaders,
> The heavy omnibus, the driver with his interrogating
>   thumb, the clank of the shod horses on the granite
>   floor . . .

Such lines as these have been multitudinously echoed in modern prose and poetry, they have been endlessly recapitulated by the journey of the realistic movie camera up the city street. One might argue that Whitman's descriptions of the city made possible T. S. Eliot's *Waste Land*. The horror of Eliot's London, as of Baudelaire's "*cité pleine de rêves*," is unknown in *Leaves of Grass*, but was not Whitman the first poet, so to speak, who put real typists and clerks in the imaginary city?

There can be no doubt that "Song of Myself" made sex a possible subject for American literature, and in this respect Whitman wrought a great revolution in, for example, his beautiful idyllic scene in which the "handsome and richly drest" woman imagines herself to join the "twenty-eight young men" who "bathe by the shore." In such a passage as this (as Henry Adams was to point out) American literature was moving toward the freedom and inclusiveness that came more naturally to Europeans—to Flaubert, or Chekhov, whose panoramic novelette *The Steppe* includes a similarly idyllic scene of bathing and sexuality. It is sex, too, although of an inverted kind, that allows Whitman to write the following unsurpassable lines in which love is at once so sublimely generalized and perfectly particularized:

> And [I know] that a kelson of the creation is love,
> And limitless are leaves stiff or drooping in the fields,
> And brown ants in the little wells beneath them,
> And mossy scabs of the worm fence, and heap'd stones,
>   elder, mullein and poke-weed.

No summary view of "Song of Myself" would be complete without reference to the elegiac tone of the concluding lines. If, as we have been saying, Whitman's poem is remarkable for its gross inclusive scope, his elegiac verse is a great act of discrimination and nicety. Where else, in the generally grandiose nineteenth-century melodrama of love and death shall we find anything like the delicate precision of these incomparable lines?

> The last scud of day holds back for me;
> It flings my likeness after the rest and true as any, on
> the shadow'd wilds,
> It coaxes me to the vapor and the dusk.
> I depart as air, I shake my white locks at the runaway
> sun,
> I effuse my flesh in eddies, and drift it in lacy jags.
> I bequeathe myself to the dirt, to grow from the grass
> I love;
> If you want me again look for me under your boot-
> soles.
> You will hardly know who I am or what I mean,
> But I shall be good health to you nevertheless,
> And filter and fibre your blood.
> Failing to fetch me at first keep encouraged,
> Missing me one place, search another,
> I stop somewhere, waiting for you.

As every poet does, Whitman asks us provisionally to accept the imagined world of his poem. It is a fantastic world in which it is presumed that the self can become identical with all other selves in the universe, regardless of time and space. Not without precedent in Hindu poetry, this central metaphor is, as an artistic device, unique in American literature, as is the extraordinary collection of small imagist poems, versified short stories, realistic urban and rural genre paintings, inventories, homilies, philosophizings, farcical episodes, confessions, and lyric musings it encompasses in "Song of Myself." Yet as heavily taxing our powers of provisional credence, as inventing a highly idiosyncratic and illusory world, "Song of Myself" invites comparison with other curious works of the American imagination—*Moby Dick*, let us say, and

The Scarlet Letter and *The Wings of the Dove*. It is of the first importance at any rate to see that Whitman's relation of the self to the rest of the universe is a successful aesthetic or compositional device, whatever we may think of it as a moral assertion.

If we look at Whitman's implicit metaphor more closely, we see that it consists in the paradox of "identity." The opening words of *Leaves of Grass*, placed there in 1867, state the paradox:

> One's-self I sing, a simple separate person,
> Yet utter the word Democratic, the word En-Masse.

In more general terms the opening lines of "Song of Myself" state the same paradox:

> I celebrate myself and sing myself;
> And what I assume you shall assume;
> For every atom belonging to me, as good belongs
> to you.

Both politically and by nature man has "identity," in two senses of the word: on the one hand, he is integral in himself, unique, and separate; on the other hand, he is equal to, or even the same as, everyone else. Like the Concord transcendentalists, Whitman was easily led in prophetic moods to generalize the second term of the paradox of identity beyond the merely human world and with his ruthless equalitarianism to conceive the All, a vast cosmic democracy, placid, without episode, separation or conflict, though suffused, perhaps, with a bland illumination. More than anything else, it is this latter tendency which finally ruined Whitman as a poet, submerging as it did, his chief forte and glory—his entirely original, vividly realistic presentation of the comedy and pathos of "the simple separate person."

What finally happens is that Whitman loses his sense that his metaphor of self vs. en-masse is a *paradox*, that self and en-masse are in dialectic opposition. When this sense is lost the spontaneously eventful, flowing, and largely indeterminate universe of "Song of Myself" is replaced by a universe that is both mechanical and vaguely abstract. Whatever, in this universe, is in a state of becoming is moving toward the All, and the self becomes merely the vehicle by which the journey is made.

In some of his best as well as in some of his worst poems, Whitman actually conceives of the self as making a journey —for example, "Song of the Open Road," "Crossing Brooklyn Ferry," and "Passage to India." In others the self journeys, as it were, not forward and outward but backward and inward, back to the roots of its being, and discovers there a final mystery, or love, comradeship, or death—for example, the *Calamus* and *Sea Drift* poems. (Notably among the latter are "Out of the Cradle Endlessly Rocking" and "As I Ebb'd with the Ocean of Life".) In "Song of Myself," however, the self is not felt to be incomplete; it has no questing odyssey to make. It stands aggressively at the center of things, "Sure as the most certain sure, plumb in the uprights, well entretied, braced in the beams." It summons the universe, "syphons" universal experience through its dilating pores, calls "anything back again when I desire it." Or the self imagines itself to be infinitely expandable and contractible (like the web of the spider in Whitman's little poem called "A Noiseless Patient Spider"), so that there is no place where at any moment it may not be, no thing or person with whom it may not merge, no act in which it may not participate. Of great importance is the fact that most of "Song of Myself" has to do not with the self searching for a final identity but with the self escaping a series of identities which threaten to destroy its lively and various spontaneity. This combination of attitudes is what gives "Song of Myself" the alternately ecstatic and gravely musing, pastoral-godlike stability one feels at the center, around which, however, the poet is able to weave the most astonishing embellishments of wit and lyric song.

This is perhaps a valid way of feeling the shifting modes of sensibility in the poem. Yet it would be wrong to attribute any clear cut structure to "Song of Myself." "The United States themselves are essentially the greatest poem," wrote Whitman in his preface. A Jacksonian Democrat, Whitman was not an admirer of federal unity, either in a nation or a poem. He was content to make his poem a loose congeries of states and half-settled territories. He was content that his poem should mirror that "freshness and candor of . . . physiognomy," that "picturesque looseness of carriage," and that "deathless attachment to freedom" which, in his preface, he attributed to his countrymen. His style would be organic; he would "speak in literature with the perfect rectitude and insouciance" of animals and growing things. Although capable of finely pictorial images, Whitman composed more by ear than by eye, and his ear being attuned to music of the looser, more variable sort, such as the Italian operas, he strung his poems together on a free melodic line and by means of motifs, voices, recapitulations, recitatives, rests, *crescendi* and *diminuendi*.

The motif of "Song of Myself" is the self taking on a bewildering variety of identities and with a truly virtuoso agility extricating itself from each one. The poem begins with the exhortation to leave the "rooms full of perfume," the "creeds and schools." Apart from conventions,

> Apart from the pulling and hauling stands what I am,
> Stands amused, complacent, compassionating, idle, unitary.

Having put society and convention behind, "What I am" finds itself in an Edenlike, early-morning world, wherein one easily observes the portentous dialectics of the universe:

> Urge and urge and urge,
> Always the procreant urge of the world.
> Out of the dimness opposite equals advance, always
>   substance and increase, always sex,
> Always a knit of identity, always distinction, always a
>   breed of life.

But of more importance is the fact that in this idyllic world the veil is lifted from the jaundiced eye, the cramped sensibility is set free, the senses and pores of the body receive the joyful intelligences dispatched to them by a friendly and providential nature. The self appears to be the offspring of a happy union of body and soul; sublime and delightful thoughts issue from the mind in the same miraculous way as the grass from the ground. Death itself is seen to be "lucky." And, in short, "what I am" can well afford to be complacent, to be certain that it is "unitary." Nor is the feeling of power denied to the self. It derives power from nature, as does the horse—"affectionate, haughty, electrical"—with which the poet compares himself. It derives power, too, from identification with others—the "runaway slave," "the butcher-boy," the "blacksmiths," "the boatmen and clam-diggers," the "trapper," the "red girl"—and finally with America itself.

> In me the caresser of life wherever moving, backward
>   as well as forward sluing,
> To niches aside and junior bending, not a person or
>   object missing,
> Absorbing all to myself and for this song.

Sections 24-28, though in places rather obscure, contain the essence of Whitman's drama of identity. The poet begins by proclaiming himself a Kosmos, and commanding

us to "unscrew the locks from the doors! / Unscrew the doors
themselves from their jambs!" so that the universe may flow
through him—"through me the current and index" (that is,
the undifferentiated flux and the "identities" that emerge
therefrom). This proclamation announces not only the un-
shakable status and palpable reality but also the redemptive
powers of the self. In a world which has been created by
banishing social sanctions and social intelligence, what will
keep man from being lost in idiocy, crime, squalor? What of
that underground realm inhabited by

> . . . the deform'd, trivial, flat, foolish, despised,
> Fog in the air, beetles rolling balls of dung?

The threat of madness, crime, and obscenity is to be allayed
by the curative powers of that Adamic world where wisdom
consists in uttering "the pass-word primeval," "the sign of
democracy." Siphoned through the haughty, electrical self or
discussed frankly by persons not inhibited by prudery (the
discourses seem perilously interchangeable), the crimes and
obscenities will be redeemed:

> Voices indecent by me clarified and transfigur'd.

The poet then records a dreamlike idyl of auto-erotic experience, in which the parts of the body merge mysteriously with
natural objects, and a great deal of diffuse and wistful love
is generated. And, when dawn comes, the redemption is symbolized in these astonishing metaphors:

> Hefts of the moving world at innocent gambols silently
>   ' rising, freshly exuding,
> Scooting obliquely high and low.
> Something I cannot see puts upward libidinous prongs,
> Seas of bright juice suffuse heaven.

The poem then speaks anew of how the self may be distorted
or destroyed. The poet's "identity" is said to be assailed and

warped into other "identities" by agents referred to as "traitors," "wasters," and "marauders." Somewhat elusive in particular, these appear to have in common a quality of aggressiveness and imperiousness. They act as a radical individualist conceives society to act. They break down the self, they swagger, they assert convention, responsibility and reason, they dominate and impose passivity and furtiveness on the individual.

The beautiful, diffuse, kindly dawn is succeeded by a more formidable, a more imperious, apparition. The "dazzling and tremendous" sun leaps over the horizon and cries, "See then whether you shall be master!" The poet replies to this challenge by saying that the sunrise would indeed "kill me / If I could not now and always send sunrise out of me." The power with which the poet defeats what seeks to destroy him is asserted to be "my vision" and "my voice."

> My voice goes after what my eyes cannot reach,
> With the twirl of my tongue I encompass worlds.

In Section 26 both the metaphorical effects and the subject matter shift from the visual to the auditory. The "bravuras of birds, bustle of growing wheat, gossip of flames, clack of sticks cooking my meals"—these and myriad other sounds amplify into a symphonic orchestration. The crescendo and dying fall of the conclusion are rendered with full tone and exquisite wit.

> I hear the train'd soprano (what work, with hers, is this?)
> The orchestra whirls me wider than Uranus flies,
> It wrenches such ardors from me I did not know I possess'd them,
> It sails me, I dab with bare feet, they are lick'd by the indolent waves,
> I am cut by bitter and angry hail, I lose my breath,

Steep'd amid honey'd morphine, my windpipe throttled
   in fakes of death,
At length let up again to feel the puzzle of puzzles,
And that we call Being.

But again the poet is confronted with "Being"—that is,
form or identity—and is not certain that this is the Being he
wants to be. It is therefore dissipated and generalized, in
Section 27, into a universal process of reincarnation.

In Section 28 there occurs the famous auto-erotic pastoral
dream in which "prurient provokers," like nibbling cows,
"graze at the edges of me." The "provokers," conceived as
symbolic of the sense of touch, arouse and madden the dream-
ing poet and then they all unite "to stand on a headland and
worry me." After touch has "quivered" him "to a new identity"—has left him confused, vexed, self-reproachful, and isolated—he proceeds in the following sections to resume a
"true," "real," or "divine" identity. This act of restoration is
accomplished through love, natural piety, pastoral and cosmic
meditations, symbolic fusions of self with America, allegations of the "deific" nature of democratic man, ritual celebrations, and fatherly preachments, and finally, in the last
Section, by the assertion that death is also merely an extrication of the self from an identity.

Everyone has noticed that the large, bland exterior of Walt
Whitman concealed a Dionysus or Pan—one of the first was
Moncure Conway, who visited Walt in Brooklyn in the summer of 1857, found him basking in the sun on a hill near the
Whitman house, and later noticed that the only decorations
in the poet's room were two engravings, "one of Silenus and
the other of Bacchus." And surely no one can read "Song of
Myself" without seeing that Whitman recreates there something of the spirit of the Greek cults out of which comedy

evolved. Does he not summon us, his boon companions, to the outdoor revel, to "dance, laugh, and sing," to celebrate the phallic god? Are not masks donned and removed, "identities" concealed and exchanged? Do we not have a ritual celebration of "Nature without check with original energy," of the cycle of death and rebirth, the *agon*, sacrifice, and *gamos* of the protagonist, i.e. the self? Do we not have in Whitman's image of the diffusion of the self in nature a religious feeling akin to that engendered in the Dionysian mysteries by the dismemberment and assimilation of the sacrificial victim?

To be sure, the "mysticism" we ordinarily associate with Whitman is less akin to Dionysian than to Oriental and Quaker religion. His mode of religious contemplation, taking it by and large, tends toward passivity and quietism. There is much of this quietism even in "Song of Myself." But the poem as a whole takes its tone from something more vital, indeterminate, violent, and primitive. And it is only to find the most appropriate name for this that one hits on the word "Dionysian." The ritual submovement of comedy asserts itself with a brilliant if spasmodic energy in "Song of Myself." It provides a metaphorical foundation for even the most elaborately artificial of verbal fancies such as "I recline by the sills of the exquisite flexible doors" or "I depart as air. I shake my white locks at the runaway sun"—lines which in point of rococo refinement rival anything that Congreve's Millamant might say to Mirabell.

Historically, Whitman's "American humor" is indeed related, however remotely, to the Restoration comedy. Broadly speaking, there have been in English since 1660 three manifestations of the comic spirit: the aristocratic high comedy of Congreve, the bourgeois sentimental or genteel comedy (by far the most pervasive and influential sort ever since the Restoration), and that American humor which has been practiced in one way or another and at one time or another by

nearly all of our best writers. This is not the place to attempt
a history of comedy or an analysis of American humor—the
latter has been done exquisitely, if a little impressionistically,
by Constance Rourke. One may merely venture the idea that,
historically, American humor is a radical modification of
sentimental comedy. At its best—in Mark Twain, Melville,
Thoreau, or Whitman—it retains the capacity of sentimental
comedy for pathos but escapes its sentimentality and its hy-
pocrisy. It achieved this by rejecting the cardinal ethical
values of bourgeois comedy—money and domestic fidelity.
American humor is contemptuous of, or at least feels remote
from, the family and money as ethical norms. In this respect
and in its tendency toward cruelty and sheer verbal brilliance
it is akin to high comedy.

Considered as a comic poem, "Song of Myself" combines
Dionysian gaiety and an impulse toward verbal artificiality
with the tone and cultural presuppositions of American humor—a striking feat of hybridization certainly, yet no more
so than that which produced *Moby Dick*. The intention here
is not to deny the justice of Emerson's remark that Whitman's poem was "a remarkable mixture of the *Bhagvatgeeta*
and the *New York Herald*" or of the voluminous but one-
sided academic scholarship which, following Emerson's remark, has regarded "Song of Myself" as an amalgam of
Oriental philosophy and American realism. The intention is
rather to shift the ground of discourse toward a more strictly
literary view—the view which Emerson also adumbrated in
his remark that the first edition of *Leaves of Grass* was an
"extraordinary piece of wit and wisdom."

In 1889 Whitman said to his Camden friends, "I pride myself on being a real humorist underneath everything else"
and when it was suggested that he might after all go down in
history as a "comedian" he replied that one "might easily
end up worse." He will certainly not go down in history as,

purely and simply, a comedian. But humor was always a strong part of his sensibility, and it is difficult to see how it ever came to be a cliché about Whitman that "he had no sense of humor." There is substantial evidence that in his early life his mind turned naturally toward comic writing. Much of his newspaper work, particularly the "Sun-Down Papers From the Desk of a Schoolmaster," which he wrote for the *Long Island Democrat* and the sketches he did for the New Orleans *Crescent* (1848) show that he had mastered at least the easier tricks of the native folk humor. At various times during the 1840's Whitman expressed in newspaper articles his partiality to Dickens and Carlyle—Dickens whom "I love and esteem . . . for what he has taught me through his writings"; Carlyle, whose *Sartor Resartus* exhibits in abundance the author's "strange wild way." From these two writers Whitman seems to have learned that a great book might be eloquent, crotchety, full of curious events and observations, or a humorous compound of realism, philosophy, and sentiment. He surely learned this even more directly from Emerson's essays. If indeed there are so many parallels between "Song of Myself" and "Self-Reliance" that we almost think the poem a versification of the essay, it is nevertheless true that the parallels are not confined to the philosophic or moral message. There is a good deal of humor in Emerson's essay of the spontaneous, odd, yeasty sort noticed by Santayana, who said that Emerson "was like a young god making experiments in creation: he botched the work and always began on a new and better plan. Every day he said, 'Let there be light,' and every day the light was new." More specifically, what Whitman may have sensed in "Self-Reliance" is the humorous touch-and-go between the self and the author, which underlies the elaborate web of portentous epigram. Surely, one of the Emersonian passages that brought the simmering Whitman to a boil (as the poet himself phrased it) was the one near the end of "Self-Reliance" where Emerson is speaking of the fatuity of foreign travel and says that although he should wake up in Naples, "there beside me is the stern fact, the sad self, unrelenting, identical, that I fled from."

But aside from the question of literary influences there is the more fundamental question of cultural influence. Whitman emulated our democratic American ideals to an extent unexampled among our great writers, and there can be no doubt that many of his moral utterances and even his poetic effects are produced by the sublime literalness of the democratic assumptions which were so faithfully registered on his plastic mind and temperament. Tocqueville (whom we shall have occasion to cite more fully in a later passage) based a part of his discussion of language and literature in the United States upon his observation that

> In democratic communities each citizen is habitually engaged in the contemplation of a very puny object, namely, himself. If he ever raises his looks higher, he then perceives nothing but the immense form of society at large, or the still more imposing aspect of mankind. His ideas are all either extremely minute and clear, or extremely general and vague; what lies between is an open void.

This habit of mind has induced in American writing a style capable of very great and sudden extremes and has drawn from such writers as Melville, Emerson, Thoreau, and Emily Dickinson their idiosyncratic styles—the common denominator among them being a tendency of the language to shift rapidly from the homely and the colloquial to a rhetoric at once highly self-conscious, highly abstract, and highly elaborate. Since such shifts of ground between incongruous extremes are of the essence of wit, it is proper to speak of wit,

or as we say, of "American humor," as a central problem in
any exact investigation of the language of American literature—so long as we keep in mind how very pervasive an attitude is American humor. For indeed this form of wit is not
confined to rural hoe-downs, minstrel shows, or tall tales
about Paul Bunyan. It is a style, a habit of thought which allows for the different combinations of the native vernacular
and traditional English created by the American authors, as
well as their common habit of shifting with such brilliant effect from the particular to the general, from the small to the
great, from the concrete to the transcendent. To encompass
such effects a language must be highly flexible, capable not of
subtle and sustained modulations, as is the prose of Edmund
Burke or the poetry of Shakespeare,* but—as Selincourt observed in writing about Whitman's language—of rapid transpositions, rapid shifts of language and of levels of discourse.
And if these remarks are generally true of all American authors, they seem more literally true of Whitman than of anyone else.

Thus Whitman's struggle for a language in the years before
1855 was not essentially different from that of his peers among
American writers. It was easy to combine the literary with
the vernacular as a joke, and Whitman often did this in his
newspaper writing, as in (a sentence from one of his New
Orleans sketches) "a beautiful, enameled, filigree, inlaid
morceau of *bijouterie*, whose value intrinsically, *per se*, was
perhaps about six bits," or "we will e'en just have to give the
go-by." It was more difficult to learn the trick of producing
similar transpositions without being silly or bathetic—such a
trick as is turned toward the end of "Song of Myself" where
the last line of Section 43 and the first of 44 are:

---

* Shakespeare's style, wrote Whitman (sounding for the moment
like Burke) is determined by "the exquisite and seductive transfiguration of caste."

Nor the present, nor the least wisp that is known.
It is time to explain myself—let us stand up.

And most difficult of all was to achieve the standard accomplishment of the poetry at its best—a style, that is, which is "literary" and conversational at the same time, a style which has one eye on the individual and the concrete and one eye on the general and the transcendent.

One had better hasten to admit that a good deal of caution is called for in arguments which adduce the culture a poet lives in to explain his aesthetics. For one thing, it is of course impossible to say just what American culture is or to be sure that one traces aright its manifold influences on poetry. Then, again, no culture is perfectly unique. France has had democratic poets, there are moments in Rabelais and Kafka which seem indistinguishable from "American humor," Heine and Arnold wrote relatively "free verse," Whitman's own ideals were not only national but international. Yet the fact remains that we do have an observable national culture as well as an inherited European one, and that a truly historical critique of Whitman's poetry must begin with a view of the spoken and unspoken assumptions, the myths and habits of mind, the manners and "sentiments," of the culture the poet lived in.

Read as autobiography "Song of Myself," like *Leaves of Grass* as a whole, seems remarkably ironic, covert, elusive, and given to skipping back and forth between the personal and the generic. Yet among Whitman's confusing attempts to describe the subject of *Leaves of Grass* there is the recurring idea that it "has been mainly the outcropping of my own emotional and other personal nature—an attempt from first to last, to put a *Person*, a human being (myself, in the latter half of the nineteenth century in America) freely, fully and truly on record." As early as the Brooklyn *Eagle* days Whitman had praised Goethe's autobiography for being a book of this sort and had held it up to his readers as an exemplary modern work. But to compare "Song of Myself" with *Dichtung und Wahrheit* or with Rousseau's *Confessions* or with Wordsworth's *Prelude* is to be struck with how sparsely Whitman has represented himself, how small is the volume of the concrete natural and social particularity of the author's life. Anyone who has read a life of Whitman can make up a long catalogue of interesting particulars which the poet never treats in his poetry. Modern readers tend to chide Wordsworth for leaving sex out of the *Prelude;* yet there is infinitely more of concrete autobiography in the *Prelude* than there is in *Leaves of Grass.* Wordsworth moves from the personal and the particular to the general with a massive inductive maneuver, Whitman leaps from the one to the other and back again with the utmost agility. His native "humor," when it is not meditative or elegiac, is, in "Song of Myself," equivalent to what Nietzsche praised as the "presto" style and which he found pre-eminently in the combined French and Latin temperament of Stendhal.

A comparison of characteristic European works such as *The Red and the Black*, the lyrics of Blake, and the *Prelude* with "Song of Myself" leads us to an important distinction. In their presentation of a natural history of the self, Stendhal, Blake, and Wordsworth trace the passage of the individual from innocence to experience, from solitude to society. They tell us that the inevitable and proper task of the individual is to transcend, although not to abandon, his innocence through *social* experience. Temperamental anarchists though these authors may sometimes be, and corrupt as they may think society is, they nevertheless believe that society is a redemptive agent, without which innocence is helpless or even culpable.

Our American literary tradition has differed radically from

the European on this point. At the heart of the fiction of such
writers as Cooper, Melville, Mark Twain, and Faulkner, as
modern criticism has often pointed out, there is "a version of
pastoral." It is a dream of innocence and freedom which invites the young man to escape society and to seek adventure
as well as the fulfillment of his moral being amid the influences and sanctions of wilderness, sea, or river. This pastoral
myth encourages the neophyte to regard women either as
seraphic creatures unsuited to the rigors of the free masculine
life or as threatening harpies who wish only to destroy the
dream of masculine freedom and subdue the male to the conventions of society. Certainly from the point of view of
Western culture the representation of women by some of the
classic American authors is a striking absurdity. Could Western culture, gazing at Cooper's Alice Munroe and Judith
Hutter, Melville's Yillah and Hautia, Hawthorne's Hilda and
Miriam, these innocent fair and sinister dark "women," believe them to be a compensation for the pang of America's
birth? The myth has, however, its own sort of love, first codi-
fied perhaps in Cooper's *Deerslayer*. Natty Bumppo's love
takes two forms, a nature mysticism (my love, says Cooper's
hero in rejecting Judith Hutter because she is sexually tainted,
is in the green foliage of the forest and the clear waters of
the lake) or the tranquil idyl of masculine companionship
(Natty and Chingachgook). Natty Bumppo, according to
Balzac "a magnificent moral hermaphrodite, born between
the savage and the civilized states of man," was a spiritual
father of Walt Whitman; he was also, as we learn from the
conversations with Traubel, one of Whitman's favorite fic-
tional characters.

Urbanite though he was, everything in Whitman's upbring-
ing and native temperament fitted him to be the devotee of
this pastoral myth. So powerfully did he feel its demands, in
fact, that in "Song of Myself" he not only celebrated his ac-

ceptance of the myth; he burst through its usual limits and transcended its usual meaning. In most of the classic American authors, society is not ultimately denied. It is merely deplored and temporarily abandoned, for in the minds of each there lurks somewhere over the horizon of the pastoral idyl a social convention. Even in treating what they take to be their most important theme, the initiation of the neophyte, Cooper, Melville, and Faulkner, intimate, despite their genuine democratic feelings, that it must occur in a context of spiritual or moral hierarchy. Cooper's *Satanstoe*, Hawthorne's *House of the Seven Gables*, Melville's *Pierre*, Faulkner's *Sound and the Fury* are firmly enough conscious of social and historical values to make them excellent dramas of the decline of families. Hawthorne and James are intensely conscious of moral obligations and moral differences. Emily Dickinson and Melville are struck by the definitive disjunctions which may exist between man and nature, or man and god, or man and fellow man. In short, the preponderant tendency of the classic American writers—despite their broad areas of commonalty with Whitman (and Emerson)—has been toward an insistence on placing the individual in a world in which inequities, distinctions, and limitations are radically present. This has implied at least a fluctuating sense of society, and if Whitman's literary peers did not make so much of society as, by and large, their European contemporaries did, they nevertheless had enough moral skepticism to keep them from supposing they could get along without it. But in "Song of Myself" Whitman does not content himself with deploring society and taking to the woods with his bachelor companions. He entirely destroys society by imaginatively transfiguring it so that it becomes, as it were, merely the particular locus of the innocent pastoral world. Society is first denounced and then poetically transfigured in such a way that it can be absorbed into the native sensations, desires, and aspirations of the nonsocial man. Whitman's mind—as exemplified in "Song of My-self"—was perfectly utopian and this is, of course, one reason why we do not freely read and enjoy his greatest poem. The modern mind has been made so fully aware of the historical tragedies implied by utopian politics that it has forgotten the distinctive human virtues of the radical utopian vision. One may add that only in his early poems is Whitman the free spirit. Although there is still some radical utopian feeling in such a later work as *Democratic Vistas*, the same impulses which find poetic expression in "Song of Myself" take on in the prose polemics of *Democratic Vistas* a conservative, pru-dential tone.

This transfiguration of society has several advantages for the poet, and Whitman has made resplendent use of them in "Song of Myself." It gives the poet an enormous and bril-liant egotism. The unfolding discoveries about himself and about what can be done poetically with his ideas about him-self provide a refreshing current of exhilaration and a scene of action which we can believe to be free of man-made limita-tions and proscriptions. The idea of perfect freedom, of the "eligibility" of the self to everything else—the nation, the cosmos, all other selves—this is the valuable illusion created by Whitman's first great poem. The insouciance, the continuous upwelling sense of novelty, the brash self-assurance which al-ternates so charmingly with grave humor and tender concern for the suffering of others and of the self—these qualities and many more save Whitman's egotism from being merely re-pellent and "rhetorical."

Granted, these are not qualities which excite our age, which is very much an age of moral gloom. Granted, too, that Whit-man's moral vision is dubious and contradictory. One must admit, furthermore, that although it has its own virtues, Whit-man's utopian version of the American pastoral myth has so far proved less artistically dependable, less suggestive of imaginative possibility than the myth as conceived by the other classic authors. And despite Whitman's much asserted Americanism, theirs seems just at present to be historically the more influential myth. As I have suggested before, Whitman achieved the remarkable feat of being an eccentric by taking more literally and mythicizing more simply and directly than anyone else the expressed intentions and ideals of our democracy. He is, in "Song of Myself," the only really "free" American. He is, or seems to be, beyond good and evil, beyond the compulsion to pit his ideals against history and social reality. Cooper, Melville, Mark Twain are never so transcendently free; their dreams are troubled and their having dreams makes them sad and guilty; they impose upon us the weary task of moral judgment and upon themselves a willed and rhetorical self-justification. And if Whitman affords a welcome contrast to our American moralists, he also floods the ego with a vital gaiety of a special quality unknown to Europe—unless, indeed, the note was struck by Nietzsche, who complains of the thinkers and scholars of his time because "thinking itself is regarded by them as something slow and hesitating, almost as a trouble, and often enough as 'worthy of the sweat of the noble'—not at all as something easy and divine, closely related to dancing and exuberance!" In "Song of Myself" there is none of that straining desperation, that gloomy, willful, grammatical Romanticism which always threatens to take the joy out of the egotism of Byron, Carlyle, and sometimes of Nietzsche himself, no sense of the fated will of the European nineteenth century urging itself toward its melodramatic suicide. And so it is possible sometimes to prefer Whitman's comic vision to the social melodrama of the European writers and the moral idyls of Whitman's compatriots, to value it separately and for what it is—a great releasing and regenerative force.

One may even suppose that future readers may find Whitman more relevant to their vital concerns than the tragic moralists among our American writers. Of these tragic moralists, with their pastoral legend, Cooper may seem the first and Hemingway the last. Yet Whitman may be regarded as more modern than Hemingway. For was it not Whitman who first sought out the grounds on which in the midst of our urban modernization the individual with all his dilemmas and aspirations can exist, whereas Hemingway still clings to a version of nineteenth-century romanticism which in Melville and Mark Twain was already nostalgic? The future reader may not think it an extreme case if someone should remark to him that Whitman's utopian rejection of society is under modern conditions the necessary first step toward the preservation of what is vital in society and the revitalization of what is not, and, furthermore, that despite his intellectual shortcomings, despite even the final disappearance of his idealism into the All, Whitman knew more of the homely root facts of the life of modern society that did Melville or Mark Twain, and that at his best his vision stubbornly began and ended with these root facts.

In his *Democracy in America* Tocqueville made certain remarkable prognostications about the qualities of imagination American writers might be expected to display when, finally, they should produce a genuinely native literature. His predictions were far from complete. He would have found much in Melville, Hawthorne, and Henry James of what he expected; but he would have found much, also, to surprise him—Melville's profound mythology, the precision of Hawthorne's art, James's love of Europe. He would have been less surprised by Emerson and hardly at all by Whitman (it is for this reason that I risk boring the reader by reciting from Tocqueville certain predictions which by now he may know all too well).

Tocqueville suggested that the newness of his society as well as his belief in equality, progress, and the perfectibility of man would deprive the American poet of most of the traditional poetic resources. He will have no received myths, Tocqueville wrote. He will have no pantheon upon which to draw, no "intermediate powers" such as aristocratic people place between God and man. He will have no wealth of historical or legendary materials, and, in fact, he will feel an "instinctive distaste for what is ancient." Not having a rich past, said Tocqueville, and distrusting such as he has, the American poet will make the future the repository of his ideals and the source of his sense of wonder and aspiration. To be sure, Whitman announces in his 1855 Preface that "America does not repel the past or what it has produced under its forms or amid other politics or the idea of castes or the old religions." Yet, as if consciously bearing Tocqueville out, he spoke of the past as "a corpse" which must make way for the future, for the future is where all "solid and beautiful forms" reside.

If democracy robs the poet of the past, Tocqueville wrote, it also, in a sense, robs him of the present. That is, he will find among his contemporaries no more individuals capable of poetic representation than he finds in myth and legend. In a society in which all men are regarded as equal none seems to invite idealization as an individual hero. "In democratic communities, where men are all insignificant and very much alike," the poet who surveys his contemporaries will instantly behold, not them, but the nation as a whole, or mankind as a whole. Or he will behold himself. And even when he sees himself, he will do so paradoxically—he will see himself, that is, as an individual and, at the same time, as a representative of the nation or of mankind. Yet this tendency, like the democratic poet's mythic idea of the future, will prove a genuine new source of poetry. "Democratic nations have a clearer perception than any other of their own aspect," wrote Tocqueville, "and an aspect so imposing is admirably fitted to the delineation of the ideal."

Even Whitman's notion of the poet as the passive recipient of inspiration who merely utters without conscious artifice the song which possesses him is to be understood as peculiarly compatible with a democratic society. For the democrat automatically assumes himself to be the fully accredited representative and spokesman of his country, and thus he is easily disposed to believe, when he becomes a poet, that his country, mankind, and the universe itself speak through him. This is the assumption of Whitman's Preface, where we read that "The greatest poet has less a marked style, and is more the channel of thoughts and things without increase or diminution." One of the paradoxes of American democracy is that though it is the product of a high civilization it is conducive to an idea of the poet which belongs rather to the age of the muses than to later periods. This is one of our ways of returning to the primitive sources of the imagination, and it operated in Whitman along with two other tendencies in the same direction—the "inner light" of the Quakers and the romantic or transcendental theory of poetic "possession."

In what sense is Whitman a mythic poet? "Great are the myths" of the past, he wrote in a poem originally included in the 1855 edition. But, he adds, great also are the myths of democracy, and the democratic poet must assert not only the myths of "the risen and fallen nations" but also Liberty, Equality, Day and Night, Truth, Language, Law, Justice, Life, and, of "the greatest purport," Death. The reader of this poem will surely reflect that if Adam and Eve, Dionysus and Zeus are the creatures of myth, we appear to be confronted with something else when Liberty and Equality (not personifications but pure abstractions) are substituted for these personages. An indispensable characteristic of myth is its air of having a past, of retaining the aura of a primitive time which either has or is imagined to have historically existed. A poem about Zeus is of no interest if it fails to recapture a sense of the primitive religious feeling. And Whitman's culture had, properly speaking, no primitive age.

Still, we are correct in thinking, as did the poet himself, that there are mythic elements in "Song of Myself," as throughout *Leaves of Grass* (although it might be well, but for the awkwardness of the phrase, to refer to Whitman's "pseudo-myths"). There is no population of glamorous or semidivine persons; but there are emergent generic persons of the kind discerned by Edward Dowden, one of Whitman's first foreign admirers, when he wrote that "the mettlesome, proud, turbulent, brash, self-asserting young Achilles, lover of women and lover of comrades, of Whitman's epic, can be no other than the American people; the Ulysses, the prudent, the 'cute, the battler with the forces of nature, the traveller in the sea-like prairie, desolate swamp and dense forest is brother Jonathan." And, as Dowden might have added, there is the self, a dramatic presence called Walt Whitman, "hankering, gross, mystical, nude."

And if "Song of Myself" invokes a future instead of a past, it nevertheless adduces a kind of generalized primitive age as it goes along. Whitman does this partly in the usual, or Virgilian, manner—he adduces legends, that is, from the national past as in the passages about the Alamo and Bunker Hill. But far more striking and pervasive is his poetically bold assertion of a flowing universe in which the primitive and the civilized seem to be interchangeable or contemporaneous. This entails, of course, an inevitable artificiality and it encourages an elaborate fancifulness—which is why the mythic elements in Whitman's poems, as in many more modern works, impress one as being contrived *ad hoc*. In a country like ancient Greece, where history reached back into a native barbarism, the most sophisticated literature could be made to reverberate a copious mythology. But the American writer, who, like Cooper, Melville, Mark Twain, Hawthorne, Parkman, Faulkner, or Hemingway, includes in his temperament the myth-making tendency, has to rely on the few modes of genuine myth-producing experience America offers—such as, the Odyssey-like whale or bear hunt or flight down the river, the frontier legends, or the deeply imbedded customs of the old South or early New England—and contrive the rest as his genius will allow. Although actually he was much more citified than any of his peers among the great American authors, Whitman shared with them Thoreau's ideas on "wildness."

Walking "west," in his sublimely imaginary manner, Thoreau reflected that "In literature it is only the wild that attracts us. Dullness is but another name for tameness. It is the uncivilized free and wild thinking in 'Hamlet' and the 'Iliad,' in all the Scriptures and Mythologies, not learned in the schools, that delights us." Whitman's poems show the tendency toward the mythic and emblematic which has transformed in American hands so many potential "novels" into "romances" and so many poems into prophecies. Yet Whitman makes much less consistent use of the available mythic motifs than he might (although the camerado on the open road might be considered a version of the Odyssey motif).

Generally speaking, Whitman's method is to mythicize the abstractions of democratic idealism. For Whitman, equality, freedom, and fraternity are pervasive and magical laws vibrantly revealed in the visible universe; and the self is a preternatural being, a numenous presence which is felt with all the wonder the primitive man feels in the presence of his god or tutelary spirit.

In the sense, then, that it mythicizes, not primitive intuitions and fundamental human dilemmas, but abstract ideas which are the product of ages of civilization, "Song of Myself" is the most contrived and artificial of American mythic fictions. There is no dramatic sense of the past, no pathos of a past being destroyed before one's eyes, as there is in the work of other American mythicists. There is no real temporal dimension in the poem. Even "the future" is more honorific, something praised and insisted on, than temporal. There is instead a kind of timeless emergence, which allows the poet to make the logically and historically preposterous but poetically valid assertion that past and present exist contemporaneously. By a vast *tour de force* Whitman makes us believe that American democracy, the product of Christianity and European enlightenment, exists in a half-urban, half-pastoral world of primeval novelty, where the blessed and unfallen inhabitants gather to hear the songs and preachments of the bard, as the people of the forest gathered about Orpheus. For this poet, the products of a high civilization—science, skepticism, evolution, the belief in equality and progress—are convertible into the images of a primeval mythic vision. (Intellectually, it must be admitted, this attitude is no different from that of countless provincial and unlettered people of our New World—those restless, aspiring, crankish persons who confuse science with magic, atheism with religion, biases and crotchets with thought, who read, as Whitman did, Voltaire, Franklin, Tom Paine, and Robert Ingersoll, who take up pseudo-sciences like phrenology, as Whitman did, and who, like Whitman in his late years, tend to confine their discussion of Shakespeare to the "Baconian controversy." Fortunately the transfiguring powers of poetry are inexhaustible.)

The national literature—witness Poe, Melville, Emerson, James—has been distinguished by its concern with the self. Our optimistic moralists and philosophers have thought of the redeemed, healthy, spontaneous self as the nearly sufficient assurance of an ever improving and one-day ideal social order. Our poets and novelists have posed the question of selfhood and made ghosts and symbols out of the self, the other self, the *doppelgänger*, the ideal self, the evil self in a great variety of ways. Yet it was left to Whitman to make of the self the new mythic principle which is one of his chief claims of originality.

As a moralist Whitman shares with Emerson his belief that the self can be self-sufficient and that merely by being good, free, various, spontaneous, and loving enough, it can extrude, as it were, the good society. Speaking of the effect upon the conception of the self entailed in the transcendentalists' view of nature, society, and the individual, Mr. Quentin Anderson has written: "Under the pressure engendered by packing nature, history, providence, creativity, and political and moral sanctions into it, the self . . . becomes a species of universal register or 'transparent eyeball' [the phrase is Emerson's], and the capacity for a dramatic, an actively social life, seems to disappear altogether." Mr. Anderson, who would doubtless extend his view to include Whitman, is right to object to what is morally speaking so hazardous an overestimation of what the unaccommodated self can accomplish.

But in "Song of Myself" Whitman's moral dubiety is his poetic plenitude. The transcendentalist trick of making the self "a species of universal register" is Whitman's triumph in "Song of Myself." Whitman's fanciful idea that the self is able to assume the imprint of any "identity" it wishes without regard to the barriers of space or time and thus to provide for the transformation of the simple separate person into the democratic en-masse or community of comrades was, as a conceit or mythic conception, a stunning novelty. It allowed him to reconstitute the mythic imagination on new ground. T. S. Eliot apparently regards Whitman's claim to originality, at least of poetic language, as spurious. But it must be noted that *The Waste Land* is not the first "universal" English poem loosely organized by a stream-of-consciousness or musical tech-

nique, having a protagonist called "I" who merges regardless
of time and space with a variety of historic and mythical
personages, and celebrating the recurring cycles of death and
rebirth—"Song of Myself" is. This thematic similarity need
not be pressed as a case of Whitman's "influence"; two poems
could hardly be more dissimilar in tone. The affinity seems
rather to be a coincidence of two very different minds asking
the same implicit question: What, in a spiritually eclectic,
already Alexandrian, "American" world, is the status and fate
of the self? It is probable, one may add, that both "Song of
Myself" and *The Waste Land* were influenced by the
Bhagavad Gita, which may be loosely described as themati-
cally similar to these two poems.

A more direct influence of Whitman is that upon Joyce.
Finnegans Wake, the culminating work, the summa of the
contemporary mythic movement in literature (and in some
ways, it must be admitted, its *reductio ad absurdum*) seems
confessedly to owe a debt to Whitman. The bard referred to
as "old Whiteman self" (p. 263) is made to say (p. 551) "I
foredreamed for thee and more than fullmaked: I prevented
for thee in the haunts that joybelled grail light-a-leaves . . ."
And indeed the "panromain* apological which Watllwe-
whistlem sang" may easily have suggested to Joyce how a work
of literature might picture "the soul of everyelsesbody rolled
into its olesoleself." Humphrey Chimpden Earwicker, Joyce's
protagonist, has the same capacity as the "I" of "Song of Myself" to merge ("at no spatial time") with and become anyone and anything in the universe. The drawer of parallels
might well begin with Sections 27-31 of "Song of Myself,"
where, for example, he will find Whitman referring to reincarnation thus:

---

* Presumably—pan-Roman (i.e., "universal") and pan-romaine (i.e.,
a vegetable: "Leaves of Grass") and pan-*roman* (the universal novel).

To be in any form, what is that?
(Round and round we go, all of us, and ever come
  back thither.)

—an interesting analogue of Joyce's "The Vico road goes
round an round to meet where terms begin." In a very real
sense, then, *Finnegans Wake* is the ultimate development of a
literary method "foredreamed" in "Song of Myself." This
fact serves to remind us that various and valuable as the
mythic movement in literature has been, it seems finally to
run into the sands and to be cherished only by a small number
of readers. It is ironic in view of Whitman's desire for a
universal audience that he should have furnished what is
from one point of view the first example of so special a kind of
literature. But it is historically significant that the affinity between Whitman and Joyce should be an affinity of comic
sensibility. The references to Whitman in *Finnegans Wake*
(brief as they are) are fresher and more moving to the modern reader than are those, for example, in Hart Crane's *The
Bridge*, where Whitman is understood only as the aspirational
prophet.

Whitman was, of course, nothing like the modern poets in
point of conscious technical sophistication. His practice was
sometimes highly sophisticated, but his theory was either
fragmentary and hesitating or nonexistent. One poetic device
which did interest him and which he reflected on at length
(doubtless with the encouragement of Emerson's essays on
Nature and the Poet) was the use of words "indirectly"—that
is, as "hieroglyphics," "symbols," or implied myths. Whitman
conceived of language as he conceived of the universe. It was a
flow—"that huge English flow," as he called it in the open
letter to Emerson which he appended to the 1856 edition of
Leaves of Grass. Words are "magical" or "spiritual" when
they first emerge, as "identities," from the flow. All words, as

he had learned from Emerson, were originally poetic metaphors. And it is the business of the bard to speak words from which the sensuous poetic and "spiritual" quality has not been lost or to revivify words from which it has. This "real first-class poet," said Whitman, reviewing his own book in 1855, has hit upon a new scheme which is more "subtle" than the presentation of "acts and events" by Homer or of "characters" by Shakespeare. "Every sentence and every passage" of this poet "tells of an interior not always seen, and exudes an impalpable something which sticks to him that reads, and pervades and provokes him to tread the half-invisible road where the poet, like an apparition, is striding fearlessly before." This transcendentalist or prophetic illusion is to be created by using words still redolent of the essence of that universal flow of unconscious thought from which all words emerge. Words, poetic thoughts, thus originate as miraculously as do the leaves of grass. Indeed, the objects of nature, particularly phallic objects, are called, in "Spontaneous Me" (1856), "real poems." Like all natural things, "all words are spiritual . . ." he wrote in *An American Primer*. And like natural things they have a history, an evolution. "Whence are they? along how many thousand and tens of thousands of years have they come? those eluding, fluid, beautiful, fleshless, realities, Mother, Father, Water, Earth, Me, This, Soul, Tongue, House, Fire."

In Whitman's view of language (which is clear, it must be admitted, only in its general outlines), colloquial words best unite the "natural" and the "spiritual." Therefore the poet will use words in such a way as to give them the freshness, raciness, and mythic significance of colloquial speech. Such seems to be Whitman's argument in his "Slang of America," an essay of especial interest in relation to "Song of Myself." Slang he understands to be "the lawless germinal element below all words and sentences, and behind all poetry," which provides "a certain perennial rankness and protestantism in speech." What he heard among the common people he took to be the genesis of poetry: "the wit—the rich flashes of humor and genius." The poet will use language as the earliest people did when colloquial words—the "living and buried speech," as he says in "Song of Myself"—were incipient myths, when they "gave the start to, and perfected, the whole immense tangle of the old mythologies." Characteristically Whitman thought of these incipient myths as having a comic element.

Thus in his ideas about words, as in his poetic practice, Whitman is paradoxically extremely civilized and extremely primitive. Both semanticist and bard, he is a kind of primitive I. A. Richards and a sophisticated Orpheus. As a poet who wishes to create a mythic poetry he is confronted with the dilemma (the democratic dilemma, Tocqueville would say) of a sensibility which quickens to mythic feeling only at opposite ends of the spectrum, either in spontaneous, inchoate, "germinal" experience or in abstractions such as Mother, Father, Equality, Love or Democracy. What he lacks, as compared with Homer, for example, or Dante or Milton, is a mediating body of mythic narrative and metaphor. All such mediating metaphors struck Whitman as "feudal" and therefore improper in democratic poetry. It was what he took to be the positive advantage of this attitude that led him to describe his poems as more "subtle" than Homer with his poetry of "acts and events" and Shakespeare with his poetry of "characters."

Having given up so much—so much more, indeed, than his democratic situation forced him to give up—Whitman is reduced to two principal stratagems of mediation—his use of words in a mythic-semantic manner, as if he were Adam naming the animals, and his one grand narrative and metaphorical image of the self with its dialectic powers and its eternal vitality and significance. Not, of course, that these stratagems

are his whole stock in trade; rather, he sets them triumphantly in opposition to the traditional techniques which
remain in his poetry and which he always found necessary but
which, nevertheless, he could never succeed with when he
used them alone. When Whitman writes badly it is either because he is trying to get along without his own stratagems (as
in "O Captain, my Captain") or because he is misusing them.
Anyone who asks sheer words to do so much cannot help
debasing the currency and sometimes producing mere lifeless
lists of names. As Matthiessen pointed out, he also runs the
risk of writing nonsense—for instance, such a line as

> O for you whoever you are your correlative body! O
>   it, more than all else, you delighting,

where his word-adducing transcends all recognizable gram-
mar and metaphor and becomes a sort of abortive verbal
algebra. And the self cannot mediate between the concrete and
the abstract when, as but too frequently happens, it is absorbed into the abstract. But in "Song of Myself" these errors
are mostly avoided, and it is in this poem that Whitman's
peculiar poetic devices work best.

So far as it is philosophical, the preceding discussion conceives of Whitman in the dualistic universe formulated for
modern times by Descartes. Broadly speaking, this dualism
was, of course, the characteristic mode of thought in the nineteenth century. It was the characteristic mode of thought of
Walt Whitman despite the implicit undermining of its twin
pillars by the romantic irrationalism and the transcendentalist revision of idealism which alternated so picturesquely in
his mind with the rationalistic materialism he inherited from
the Enlightenment. Despite the "merging" and "identifying"
tendencies of the poet, despite the timeless, flowing universe
he speaks of, he preserves, as we have noticed at some length,
his modes of distinction and "extrication." On the whole he

operates on the ordinary assumption of his time that a poem expresses the self of the poet and reports facts from the world of nature and is therefore more or less continuous with these orders of reality. (Indeed in some of his utterances Whitman took an unusually low view of poetry, stating in various ways that he thought it a poor substitute for reality.) It should also be noted that he tended to think of language as expressing a dualistic universe, as when he says that slang words, being more poetic than other words, unite the "natural" and the "spiritual." So that it would seem that a critical language involving myth, semantic, mediation, dialectic, mind vs. matter, abstract vs. concrete, and so on, is largely adequate to a discussion of Whitman's poetry.

Largely but not perfectly. We now begin to understand the unique "transcendentalist" quality of the classic American authors, from Poe to Melville and Whitman, not only as an attempt to respond to that dualistic view of things which, as Tocqueville noted, was exacerbated by the stark oppositions of American life, but as a putative adventure in the subversion and revision of categories so as to free poetry from its subservience to the personality of the poet and to external reality and to reconstitute it as an autonomous process which discovers and even creates its own reality. Language, according to this view, is an omnivorous but transfiguring and noetic power which destroys and absorbs other orders of reality but justifies itself by furnishing "a stage where the lost worlds of self and nature are reborn as actors in the drama of meaning." Mr. Charles Feidelson, whose words these are, argues instructively in his *Symbolism and American Literature* that various versions of this "language experiment" are to be seen in all the great writers of the pre-Civil War period. Much indebted to Mr. Feidelson, I essay the following brief discussion of Whitman's "language experiment" because it seems of considerable interest and despite the fact that such an inquiry is a little outside the scope of a book which intends to be less a technical study than a cultural or historical appreciation.

There is no doubt that Whitman had in abundance the symbol-seeing capacity of the Puritan-transcendentalist mind. Relatively speaking, one finds a large number of real toads in his imaginary garden, yet he could not help seeing what he called in *Democratic Vistas* "the shows and forms of Nature" as well as nature itself. He often refers to natural objects as "words" or "thoughts." But his view of symbols is not confined to a semantic view; he is not content to understand symbols as mere static signs. Words are spontaneous, creative agents. To set a word in motion by putting it in a poem is to set it off on a career of discovery and creation. Even before he wrote "Song of Myself" Whitman had jotted down in his notebook (doubtless after reading Emerson) that "from each word, as from a womb, spring babes that shall grow to giants and beget superber breeds upon the earth." The spirit of his poetry, as he said, is "the spirit of life in visible forms."

One of the remarkable and problematic results of the absorption of the self and of nature into a purely linguistic order of reality is of course the tendency of the symbolistic poet to abolish what has traditionally been understood as subject matter. It follows that the symbolistic poem tends to be its own subject matter; the poem becomes a "drama of meaning" whose plot is the gradual discovery of an inherent significance or is in some other way a symbolization of the poetic process. This effect is sometimes produced in Whitman's poems; nearly all the best ones speak at some point of the emergent "word" or meaning and imply that the poem has to do with the visionary search for meaning. Thus, as an analogue to what was referred to above as the *tour de force* by which in "Song of Myself" Whitman posits a paradoxically urban-pastoral world of primeval novelty, a world dynamic, eventful and timeless, one may note the *tour de force* by which we are sometimes given the sensation of being afloat in a realm of symbols which is made indeterminate and exciting by the comic metamorphoses, the mergings and extrications, of the self, of nature, and of language; sometimes everything seems to have been merged in "the endless unfolding of words"—even the grass is referred to as "uttering tongues."

One observes this merging process in the tendency of the self in Whitman's poem to become identified with the process of poetic creativity. For if it is true, as was argued above, that Whitman assigns to the self a dialectic task of reconciling opposites, he is identifying it with the imagination and its classic task, so that there is a sense in which the imagination is the subject of "Song of Myself." And if the self, as Mr. Anderson says (quoting Emerson), is a "transparent eyeball" and is therefore incapacitated in its indiscriminate passivity as a moral agent, it nevertheless may retain its seeing power and behave actively in a context of emergent symbolic meaning. If, as we have seen, Whitman identified the "infinite and omnigenous self" with the unconscious, it need only be assigned the task of creating meaning in order to be identified with the imagination.

In the same paragraph in which he contrasted his poetry with that of Homer and Shakespeare, Whitman wrote:

> The theory and practice of poets have hitherto been to select certain ideas or events or personages, and then describe them in the best manner they could, always with such ornament as the case allowed. Such are not the theory and practice of the new poet.

In maintaining that the new poet is more "subtle" than Homer and Shakespeare because his poetry "pervades and provokes" the reader "to tread the half-invisible road where the poet, like an apparition, is striding fearlessly before," he was speaking of the prophetic function of the new poet but also of his "symbolistic" function. And indeed Whitman's poems may often be profitably discussed as "dramas of meaning," although to discuss them only in this manner would seem an intolerable specialization.

Many passages in "Song of Myself" play with the idea of meaning: "Do you guess that I have some intricate purpose?" or "To me the converging objects of the universe perpetually flow, All are written to me, and I must get what the writing means." The poem revels in the infirm, shifting status of all its constituents, and these are often understood as the constituents of knowledge itself. One can read "Song of Myself" as Mr. Feidelson reads Melville's *Confidence Man*—as "a comedy of human thought" and noting the fact that the confidence man's "masquerade" is analogous to the vicissitudes of the self in Whitman's poem and that in both works (different as they are in mood) one encounters a world of "inconclusive creativity," of "ceaseless fusion and disintegration" (as Mr. Feidelson says in speaking of *The Confidence Man*), a world in which meanings are incongruous, fluid, and absurd. To speak of later poems for a moment, one may doubt the usefulness of a symbolistic reading of "Out of the Cradle Endlessly Rocking"; its subject is the origin of the poet's poetry, to be sure, but the genesis of the "word" is sought naturalistically. "As I Ebb'd with the Ocean of Life," however, is in one sense a symbolistic obverse to "Song of Myself," being a despairing, rather than a joyous, response to the idea that knowledge is undependable. And there is good reason to say, as Mr. Feidelson does, that if the true subject of "Lycidas" is the Poet, that of "When Lilacs Last in the Dooryard Bloom'd" is the poetic process. The fact remains, however, that if such a poem as "Song of Myself" is a "comedy of human thought," the stage on which the most vivid actions are played out is psychological rather than epistemological. The characteristic action is the interplay, not of meaning and unmeaning, but of consciousness and unconsciousness. The pleasure of the poem consists in our watching, in the poem, the conscious mind as it confronts so awe-inspiring an array of novel and incongruous images from the waking dream life of the poet.

Illuminating in detail, a symbolistic approach to literature seems in the long run doomed to be insulative and disheartening, in spite of its commitment to the dangerous voyage into undiscovered realms of meaning. A symbolistic reading establishes interesting lines of filiation, beyond those noted above, between "Song of Myself" and those works of modern literature which find their ultimate implications in *Finnegans Wake*. But like all works of art these seem to wither before our eyes to the extent that we see them only as forms irreparably severed from the imperishable sources of being.

CHAPTER III

ASSERTIONS AND DOUBTS

WHITMAN'S CAREER between the first edition of his poems in 1855 and his departure, in 1862, for Washington is marked by a sharp contrast between the defiant self-assertiveness with which it begins and the nagging doubts, confusions, and profound melancholy with which it ends. One has the sense, in these years, of a poet who was somewhat overwhelmed by his own genius, committed now to public display, and of a man uncertain as to where his personal temperament was leading, or should lead, him. In the 1856 edition of *Leaves of Grass* there is a rather nervously assertive attempt to put the house in order, to impress upon the public that the poems are intelligible and have behind them a large-scale program. The underlying nervousness becomes more and more apparent in the late fifties, and the 1860 edition contains poems like "As I Ebb'd with the Ocean of Life," in which the whole "program" seems entirely dissipated in a profound and pervasive doubt which goes to the very root of being. If in 1856 Whitman was his own St. Paul, by 1859 he had become his own Job. Yet both the advocate and the afflicted doubter could speak in the accents of great poetry.

From every worldly point of view the 1855 edition was a spectacular failure. Most of its few readers convicted *Leaves of Grass* on grounds of incomprehensible language, obscenity, barbarism, or a vulgar materialism which was content with

99

drawing up lists of things and uttering crude exclamations. There were, to be sure, more sophisticated responses—a rather lofty notice by Charles Eliot Norton and a more appreciative one by Edward Everett Hale, who spoke of the genuine freshness and novelty of the poet's vision.

The most celebrated response to Whitman's volume was, of course, Emerson's letter. Whitman could prize it all the more because some of the well-known writers to whom he sent copies had summarily sent them back or left them unacknowledged. And one, no less a personage than Whittier, is said to have thrown his copy into the fire. So remarkable (though perhaps so familiar) a letter must be set before the reader in full.

Concord, Massachusetts, 21, July, 1855

Dear Sir—I am not blind to the worth of the wonderful gift of *Leaves of Grass*. I find it the most extraordinary piece of wit and wisdom that America has yet contributed. I am very happy in reading it, as great power makes us happy. It meets the demand I am always making of what seemed the sterile and stingy Nature, as if too much handiwork, or too much lymph in the temperament were making our Western wits fat and mean.

I give you joy of your free and brave thought. I have great joy in it. I find incomparable things said incomparably well, as they must be. I find the courage of treatment which so delights us, and which large perception only can inspire.

I greet you at the beginning of a great career, which yet must have had a long foreground somewhere, for such a start. I rubbed my eyes a little, to see if this sunbeam were no illusion; but the solid sense of the book is a sober certainty. It has the best merits, namely, of fortifying and encouraging.

I did not know until I last night saw the book adver-

tised in a newspaper that I could trust the name as real
and available for a post-office. I wish to see my bene-
factor, and have felt much like striking my tasks and
visiting New York to pay you my respects.

R. W. Emerson

One of the best brief criticisms of Whitman ever written and
also one of the celebrated "recognitions" in the history of
American literature, this letter cannot but remind us how few
these recognitions have been and how fortunate Whitman
was in Emerson's response.

In the fall of 1855 Whitman retired to the restful seclusion
of eastern Long Island, making one of his many withdrawals.
He may well have felt the dismay and disappointment of his
failure, the failure of a poet who wished to speak to and for a
whole people, but who might already suspect that he was
doomed to be ignored or contemned by the "En-masse" and
applauded, if at all, only by a coterie. No doubt the letter
from Emerson was frequently drawn from the pocket where
Whitman proudly kept it and that it helped him, as much as
did his rustication, to gain the new found vigor which is
apparent in the new edition of his poems he was already
beginning to plan.

The new edition appeared in the late summer of 1856. It
was brought out by Fowler and Wells, the phrenological
publishers. The name of the firm did not appear in the book,
however, and the publisher, fearing Whitman's growing noto-
riety, soon disclaimed all responsibility in the venture. On its
spine the volume bore the (unauthorized) legend "I greet
you at the beginning of a great career. R. W. Emerson." An
appendix contained favorable reviews of the first edition,
Emerson's letter, and a long reply to Emerson which most
readers have been correct in finding a somewhat mawkish
combination of hollow rhetoric and patent self-doubt. Ad-
dressing Emerson as "dear Friend and Master," the poet says

that the thirty-two poems of the new edition must constitute his long-delayed reply to Emerson's praise. Emerson and the world at large are told that the thousand copies of the first edition "readily sold," that in the present edition there are "several thousand copies," and that in a few years "the average annual call for my Poems" will be "ten or twenty thousand copies—more, quite likely." Whitman was lying about the past, exaggerating the present, and indulging in pitiful illusions about the future. The poet seemed no longer to be "aplomb in the midst of irrational things," at least to the eye which could see through the surface. Yet for all its hollowness and its air of having been written by a faithful but second-rate disciple of the Emersonian creed, the open letter makes its impressive declaration that to be a poet is the author's fate.

The showpieces of the second edition were "Song of the Open Road" and "Crossing Brooklyn Ferry." Although ultimately diffuse and tending to run out into the universal, "Song of the Open Road" makes the laudable attempt to render the universal through the self, through a putative allegory of progress, and through an idea of free will. The poet recognizes his problem—to find "objects that call from diffusion my meanings and give them shape." And any technical account of the poem must suppose that Whitman rather invokes than captures and uses these objects.

A remark by Thoreau about the 1856 edition in general seems particularly applicable to "Song of the Open Road." "By his heartiness and broad generalities," said Thoreau of Whitman, "he puts me into a liberal frame of mind prepared to see wonders,—as it were, sets me upon a hill or in the midst of a plain,—stirs me well up, and then—throws in a thousand of brick." "Song of the Open Road" is not excessively laden with "brick" (a reference to the famous "catalogues"), but there is nevertheless some disparity between what we are led to expect and what the vision actually shows us.

Although we must agree with Lawrence that Whitman's transformation of the soul from a covert thing to be sought "above" or "within" into "a wayfarer down the open road" was a great liberating act, it remains true that Whitman "seizes the soul by the scruff of her neck and plants her down among the potsherds" more effectively in "Song of Myself" than in "Song of the Open Road"—this latter being a poem which lacks an adequate stock of "potsherds" and succeeds less in representing than in declaring itself in favor of the open road.

Nevertheless the declarations themselves are so vigorous and eloquent that one is often glad to have them for what they are:

> Allons! with power, liberty, the earth, the elements!
> Health, defiance, gayety, self-esteem, curiosity;
> Allons! from all formules!
> From your formules, O bat-eyed and materialistic
>   priests.

This impulse to provisional experiment and liberation, as well as the announcement that here, on the open road,

>   is realization,
> Here is a man tallied—he realizes here what he has in
>   him,

makes Whitman's poem a classic statement of American pragmatism. And it was to this strain in Whitman that William James reacted when he exclaimed, in answer to Santayana's attack on the poet, that Whitman was "in the line of mental growth, and those who insist that the ideal and the real are dynamically continuous are those by whom the world is to be saved."

One of the peculiarities of American literature is that on the whole it has been aware of only one philosophical question—namely, necessity vs. free will. This is a considerable limitation, to be accounted for by the Calvinist heritage and our American social disposition—which has so sharply set the individual off against society, and by failing to provide those mediating ideas and agencies natural to an aristocratic order, has produced a habit of mind favorable to the philosophical preoccupation of which I speak. Like the opening pages of *Moby Dick*, like *Huckleberry Finn,* and the early chapters of *Roughing It,* and like such a lesser work as Frost's "The Lone Striker," "Song of the Open Road" is a celebration of free will, a confident assertion that whatever happens one can always (as Huck Finn says) "light out for the territory." Whitman asserted free will with the utmost exuberance, and indeed he entertained no strong idea of necessity at all. With our contemporary tendency to insist on a religious or tragic view of life, we easily make this a sufficient reason for rejecting Whitman. But can one, after all, imagine Whitman *with* an idea of necessity? Lacking the philosophical subtlety of Edwards, or Melville, and the moral subtlety of Hawthorne, he would doubtless have been as tiresome and clumsy an advocate of necessity as the "naturalist" school, which includes Dreiser and O'Neill. If Whitman's idea of free will is naïve, it can nevertheless produce that inspired wit which makes parts of "Song of the Open Road" as good as "Song of Myself":

> Why are there men and women that while they are
>   nigh me the sunlight expands my blood?
> Why when they leave me do my pennants of joy sink
>   flat and lank?
> Why are there trees I never walk under but large and
>   melodious thoughts descend upon me?
> (I think they hang there winter and summer on those
>   trees and always drop fruit as I pass;).

But although "Song of the Open Road" has comic effects, these do not determine the tone of the poem as they do in

"Song of Myself." The central metaphor is of the self in motion through a miraculous but rather sparsely populated universe. Thus the tone is more purely lyric than it could be in "Song of Myself," wherein the self "loafes" in one spot while it imaginatively expands and contracts through a thickly populated universe which provides for surprising identifications, odd juxtapositions, and interesting incongruities. As early as "Song of the Open Road" Whitman was abandoning his most original poetic discoveries and cultivating those that were less original. This tendency must be attributed partly to the pressures of public failure and to Whitman's prudent desire to make his poems more generally acceptable. "Song of the Open Road" is a quasi-traditional poem, calling to mind Oriental and medieval European visions of the path of the soul to its divine fulfillment. The poem's feeling of mingled naturalism and aspiration, though unmistakably Whitmanesque, is closer than anything in "Song of Myself" to a standard nineteenth-century sensibility. And if the sense of the American frontier is behind the poem, so too is the aspiring skylark of Shelley, the young Wordsworth blissfully alive in the dawn of youth and modernity, and (a favorite book of Whitman) George Sand's *Consuelo*.

"Song of the Open Road" does not offer us a complete moral vision of things, being so willfully optimistic. Still one hardly need share Lawrence's equally willful belief that the "open road" terminates covertly in death rather than in a free and enhanced life. We may not wish to "merge" with things with such sinking ecstasy as Whitman appears to feel in this poem. But the poem does not argue extinction by "sympathy" and identification. It urges separations as well as "mergings" and it locates death elsewhere than at the end of the road for the road is endless and the journey eternal. Death is in human convention and the corruption and denial of the self:

No husband, no wife, no friend, trusted to hear the
    confession,
Another self, a duplicate of everyone, skulking and hid-
    ing it goes,
Formless and wordless through the streets of the cities,
    polite and bland in the parlors,
In the cars of railroads, in steamboats, in the public
    assembly,
Home to the houses of men and women, at the table,
    in the bedroom, everywhere,
Smartly attired, countenance smiling, form upright,
    death under the breast-bones, hell under the skull-
    bones,
Under the broadcloth and gloves, under the ribbons
    and artificial flowers,
Keeping fair with the customs, speaking not a syllable
    of itself,
Speaking of anything else but never of itself.

Not entirely successful as a poem, "Song of the Open Road"
is nevertheless a great exemplum of the American spirit and
of this spirit not only in its crude, boosting aspect. If the vital
but often blunt-minded William James could cherish Whitman's open road, so too, we make no doubt, could his more
discriminating brother. It is striking, at any rate, how completely Henry James, through whatever process of cultural
affinity, recapitulates in *The Portrait of a Lady* the fable of
Whitman's poem. In her Jamesian language Isabel Archer re-
echoes Whitman's "I take to the open road, / Healthy, free
the world before me." She might have said, "Here a great personal deed has room. . . . Here is realization. . . . Allons!
we must not stop here." Metaphorically the novel operates
like the poem, among images of openness, vitality, and motion, of closure, sterility, and stasis. Isabel argues against
Mme. Merle that the self is sacred and she comes to her sad
end because she mistakes Gilbert Osmund for a genuine

custodian of selfhood, vitality, and noble freedom, whereas Osmund is actually "death under the breast-bones" and grinds her in the mill of convention. In James's novel Whitman's open road metaphor finds its most exquisite representation.

In considering "Crossing Brooklyn Ferry," one does not have to look for the perfect representation of its underlying metaphor anywhere but in the poem itself; surely it is one of the best Whitman wrote. Thoreau appears to be on solid ground in expressing his preference for this poem and for "Song of Myself." In "Song of the Open Road" Whitman had been seeking a less witty, more purely lyric expression of the exuberance which was one of his strong points and to expand it into the scope of vision and prophecy. In "Crossing Brooklyn Ferry" he brings a new lyric austerity and control to his capacity for pathos and musing reflection.

Everything conspires to the advantage of the poem. The river, the sea, always called out the best in a poet whose emotions were as languid, powerful, and recurrent as the tides and whose flowing depths were modified by an incorrigible gamesomeness; he was like the profound river, which "frolicked on" with its "crested and scallop-edg'd waves." The river is the perfect symbol for the "float forever held in solution" from which "identities" are "struck," just as the objects visualized in "mast-hemm'd Manhattan" and in Brooklyn, as well as the gulls and boats dropping downstream, are perfect symbols of "identity." Nor is the river less adequate as the mighty, primitive power across whose contrary tides the ferry carries man to eternity—which, the poem asserts, is the locus of everything that brings men into harmony or serves as the principle of the continuity of human feelings in space and through time.

It is usually a good sign when Whitman begins overtly to doubt himself, since his capacity for meditative self-doubt leads him to write some of his best poems, notably "Out of the Cradle," although, to be sure, self-doubt could also lead him to mere compensatory rhetoric. In "Crossing Brooklyn Ferry" the musing confession of weakness and uncertainty finds its first full voice, and it becomes a saving grace in the poem:

> It is not upon you alone the dark patches fall,
> The dark threw its patches down upon me also;
> The best I had done seem'd to me blank and suspicious;
> My great thoughts as I supposed them, were they not in
>   reality meagre?
> Nor is it you alone who know what it is to be evil,
> I am he who knew what it was to be evil,
> I too knitted the old knot of contrariety,
> Blabb'd, blush'd, resented, lied, stole, grudg'd,
> Had guile, anger, lust, hot wishes I dared not speak,
> Was wayward, vain, greedy, shallow, sly, cowardly,
>   malignant,
> The wolf, the snake, the hog, not wanting in me,
> The cheating look, the frivolous word, the adulterous
>   wish, not wanting,
> Refusals, hates, postponements, meanness, laziness, none
>   of these wanting.

The technical superiority of "Crossing Brooklyn Ferry" is in the comparative austerity of the diction and the felicity of the images—the river, the tides, the ferry boat, the sunset, the circling gulls, the ships with their tall masts, the hills on the shore, the flags and pennants. In this poem Whitman has found the "objects" he groped for in "Song of the Open Road." In alleging that these objects—the "dumb beautiful ministers"—mediate between man and eternity, Whitman has made them mediate between the uncompleted particulars of the poem and the fixed perfection of poetic form.

Both "Song of the Open Road" and "Crossing Brooklyn

Ferry" benefit by Whitman's peculiar affinity for images of
motion, his capacity to capture the sensation he himself cherished in his rambles about Long Island, his observation of
birds in flight, and of sail boats on the Sound, his inveterate
ferry boat and horse-car riding. "Crossing Brooklyn Ferry,"
allowing him to associate images of motion with the sea and
the river, called for exactly that kind of supple, indolent,
flowing motion which Whitman could supremely render. F. O.
Matthiessen cites Coleridge to the point; Whitman usually
fails, Matthiessen writes "when his verbal imagery is vio-
lently active, and only when it is more supple succeeds in en-
dowing his poetry, with the sensuousness that Coleridge held
indispensable to insure a 'framework of objectivity.' Such a
framework, in turn, is essential for 'that definiteness and ar-
ticulation of imagery, and that modification of the images
themselves, without which poetry becomes flattened into
mere didactics of practice, or evaporated into a hazy, un-
thoughtful day-dreaming.' " As a measure of Whitman's relative success and failure in his more lyric mode—for example,
in "Crossing Brooklyn Ferry" and "Song of the Open Road"
—this could hardly be improved on.

If any one poem of Whitman's can be more confidently alleged than the others in refutation of Santayana's attack on
"the poetry of barbarism," it is "Crossing Brooklyn Ferry."
Admitting for a moment the dubious idea that Santayana's
attack on Whitman's *philosophy* is a legitimate attack on his
poetry, one must believe that the assault is indeed formidable. But like other critics Santayana sees only one side of
Whitman, the primitive bard who turned to live with the
animals, the naïve, indolent, rustic whose style "reproduces
the method of a rich, spontaneous, absolutely lazy fancy."
This was Whitman's way of being a "barbarian"—that is, "a
man who regards his passions as their own excuse for being;
who does not domesticate them either by understanding their

cause or by conceiving their ideal goal." There will always be a sense in which one must attend to Santayana's denunciation of the nineteenth-century romantic naturalists, among whom he places Whitman. It is true that they often do wind up— Hegel, Browning, even Nietzsche—by merely worshipping the brute nature they had apparently been bent on observing from a firmly constituted realm of ideal values. It is true that the life of reason depends on living in some way in the two-story, Platonic-materialist world of Santayana. Yet the life of reason is only up to a point the life of poetry. And judged from the philosophical point of view, such a poem as "Crossing Brooklyn Ferry" seems adequately to provide and perfectly to constitute both nature and the ideal, to create a world in which, as Whitman says, the things of nature "furnish" their "parts toward eternity." But Santayana's essay will always be valuable. It is contemptible only in one sentence— "Even during the civil war, when he heard the drum-taps so clearly, he could only gaze at the picturesque and terrible aspect of the struggle, and linger among the wounded day after day with a canine devotion; he could not be aroused either to clear thought or to positive action." A certain elegant callousness is the price of Santayana's admirable philosophy, as naïve philosophy is the price of Whitman's poetry.

Although it contained some of Whitman's best verse, the 1856 *Leaves of Grass* was scarcely more successful than the first edition, and Whitman returned momentarily to newspaper work, becoming in 1857 editor of the Brooklyn *Times*. That Whitman was continually musing about his poetry and planning a new edition is indicated by a resolve he wrote down in June 1857, shortly after taking the job with the *Times*:

> The great construction of the new Bible. Not to be diverted from the principal object—the main life—the

three hundred and sixty-five. . . . It ought to be ready
in 1859.

He had, in other words, responded to public neglect and dis-
favor by working out in his mind the plan (in so far as it
can be said to have one) of *Leaves of Grass* as the modern
reader knows it. He would give to the world an inspired collection of poems, containing diverse elements doubtless, but
unified by a central prophetic vision. It was to be the year-
book of the people containing, one gathers, a poem for each
day—a kind of saints' calendar of democracy. It was in the
third (1860) edition that "the New Bible" took on the essential "Construction" of the later editions, though it was not
finally settled until the seventh. (The fact is, of course, that
the interior arrangement of *Leaves of Grass* has never meant
much to its readers. Nor is there any reason why it should,
since all of Whitman's attempts at formal structure never
transcended the most obvious devices—such as placing summary poems like "Starting from Paumonok" at the beginning
of the book or of one of the sections of the book; arranging
the sections, sometimes logically, sometimes whimsically, according to subject matter; sprinkling a great number of short
or incidental poems here and there; and ending with the
poem called "So Long." There is no total unifying principle in *Leaves of Grass* more precisely specifiable than "atmosphere" and one is no less astonished at the elaborate arranging and rearranging of a few good poems and many
inferior ones that finally produced *Leaves of Grass* than one
is in contemplating the similar evolution of Wordsworth's
Poems.)

   Although in June of 1857 Whitman would seem to have
embarked upon a time of prosperous productivity—having
both a salary and a new feeling for his poetry, as well as
a new and lively Bohemian social life which he took up at

this time at Pfaff's beer cellar—actually he was entering upon dark and troubled days. The student of Whitman may well be as discouraged by the paucity of facts concerning this period as he is tantalized by his stubborn sense of its cardinal importance in understanding Whitman and his poetry. Whitman himself remained reticent or cryptic about the years immediately preceding the publication of his greatest poems— the years just before 1855 and those just before 1860. And we must content ourselves with trying to perceive the general course of events during these obscure passages in his life.

On the evidence of the poetry one may trace an imaginary line, on the scale of buoyancy and self-confidence, which begins with "Song of Myself," ascends from this high point to one even higher in "Song of the Open Road" and then gradually sinks, almost out of sight, to the despair expressed in the *Sea Drift* poems. In "Song of Myself" the self is able to appropriate the power and splendor of the nation and even of the universe it celebrates. "Identity" is for the moment superbly established. By 1856, however, something has already gone wrong with the poet, and if the assertion of self and identity is even more striking than before, the assertion is nevertheless made more by the strength of will, if "Song of the Open Road" is our criterion, than by grace of the imagination. In 1859 the poet who speaks in "Out of the Cradle" is hurt and uncertain; he has turned back upon himself to the origins of his being; he is less sure of the ability of the self to absorb power from the universe than of the final victory of the universe over the self. If, as Frederik Schyberg puts it, Whitman had asked in 1855 to be sought under our boot-soles, he is still there in 1859, "but no more as the sprouting grass at the reader's feet, now only a chance bit of wreckage thrown up on the shore of existence."

The scanty—and perhaps misleading—biographical evidence induces one to think that Whitman had taken up a life of possibly general dissipation and probably of homosexual attachment. Whitman was always abnormally concerned with health. He had also an innate Quaker abstemiousness. One may therefore doubt whether he was ever capable of a life of debauchery. Yet presumably we must give some credence to the dissipations suggested in his famous resolution of April 18, 1861:

> I have this hour, this day resolved to inaugurate a sweet, clean-blooded body by ignoring all drinks but water and pure milk—and all fat meats, late suppers—a great body—a purged, cleansed, spiritualized invigorated body.

The homosexuality, however diffuse and sublimated, of the years between 1857 and 1860 seems more certain because more native to the poet than does the dissipation. There is no reason to suppose that we are not introduced to the inner chambers of Whitman's emotional world by, for example, the letter of March 19, 1863 (quoted above) which the poet dispatched from Washington to his friends of the then by-gone Pfaff days. There is genuine gaiety in this letter. There is doubtless also an aura of that "benignity" and "sweetness" which Howells had observed in Whitman when the two met in 1860 at Pfaff's. For, making his way among the young men —a "cult," says Howells—who surrounded the poet he had shaken the hand which Whitman reached out "to me, as if he were going to give it to me for good and all."

But all was not well with the convivial habitué of Pfaff's. So much is clear, though it is impossible to say whether his troubles arose because under the surface he was desperately confused and worried—"provoked," as he said in the poems —rather than genuinely homosexual or, as is often conjectured, because he had been disappointed in love or lost a lover. If Whitman's dark night was somewhat luridly flawed by artificial illuminations, that was because he was in a nineteenth-century metropolis and in his own chaste way was sharing the experience of writers like Poe and Baudelaire. Felicitously enough from the symbolic point of view Pfaff's was underground, and an interesting bit of doggerel Whitman wrote at some time during this period takes advantage of the fact.

> The vault at Pfaff's where the drinkers and laughers
>   meet to eat and drink and carouse,
> While on the walk immediately overhead pass the
>   myriad feet of Broadway,
> As the dead in their graves are underfoot hidden,
> And the living pass over them, recking not of them. . . .
> The curious appearance of the faces—the glimpse of
>   the eyes and expressions as they flit along,
> (O you phantoms! oft I pause, yearning to arrest some
>   of you!
> Oft I doubt your reality whether you are real—I sus-
>   pect all is but a pageant.)

For a brief moment at least Whitman was exemplifying the life of more modern bourgeois intellectuals, combining as he did the attitudes of the burly, proletarian radical with those of the urban aesthete and bohemian. Out of this uneasy amalgam there issued the notable poems of the 1860 edition of *Leaves of Grass*—the *Children of Adam* and *Calamus* poems, as well as "Out of the Cradle Endlessly Rocking" and "As I Ebb'd with the Ocean of Life."

The modern reader is likely to be more amused than shocked by the once notorious *Children of Adam* poems, which before the turn of the century aroused so many passions and called forth so much turgid polemic. One must agree with the general critical view that Whitman's celebrations of the body and of procreation are fatally lacking in emotion. The *Children of Adam* poems came from the pen of one for whom the love of man for woman was remote and theoretical, however much he may have been in favor of it.

A poet cannot celebrate heterosexual love without insisting on certain differences between what Whitman called "the male" and "the female." *Leaves of Grass* never celebrates heterosexual love until "the male" has been imagined as a kind of physical-culture but nevertheless bodiless titan who drinks nothing but water and bathes every day and "the female" has been imagined to be as nearly as possible like "the male," except that she "exhales" a "divine nimbus" and is a procreative machine.

Even in these bad poems Whitman does not entirely lose his characteristic power of evoking a sense of primitive novelty. For a moment we are moved by this new Adam who invites us to "behold my resurrection after slumber" and asks us to feel "the quivering fire" that plays through human limbs. And for a moment we sense Whitman's power of pathos when he projects human feelings into the universe, when sexual passion, though grown impersonal and diffuse, is yet recaptured in natural images: "the smell of apples and lemons . . . the pairing of birds . . . the wet of woods . . . the lapping of waves." But of course he has done all this infinitely better in other sections of *Leaves of Grass*. In the *Children of Adam* poems the primeval Adam is at best a shaky and flustered lover:

> O to draw you to me, to plant on you for the first time
> the lips of a determin'd man.

In these poems the genuinely pathetic tends all too easily to become the merely diffuse, and ideality becomes mere abstraction. The "new garden" to which Whitman summons "the West, the great cities" in *Children of Adam* is theoretically as interesting as the "new city of Friends" proposed by the *Calamus* poems, but it is much more remote from the best qualities of Whitman's vision.

The "dear love of comrades," which is proclaimed in the *Calamus* poems, is tenderly felt and conceived with arduousness of spirit. "The way is suspicious, the result uncertain, perhaps destructive," but the way is also mysteriously beautiful and the fulfillment genuine. If the *Children of Adam* poems remain abstract, the *Calamus* group benefits from the characteristic power of Whitman's sensibility to dilate and retract between the personal and the universal, the human and the natural, the instinctive and the utopian. These poems, we are told, are the most intimately confessional of all:

> Here the frailest leaves of me and yet my strongest
> lasting,
> Here I shade and hide my thoughts, I myself do not
> expose them,
> And yet they expose me more than all my other poems.

Yet among these shaded and hidden thoughts is a utopian vision of the future democracy:

> I dream'd in a dream I saw a city invincible to the
> attacks of the whole of the rest of the earth,
> I dream'd that was the new city of Friends,
> Nothing was greater there than the quality of robust
> love, it led the rest,
> It was seen every hour in the actions of the men of
> that city,
> And in all their looks and words.

On the whole the underlying erotic feeling of the *Calamus* poems, established symbolically by the phallic calamus-root, the image of the pond-water and of death, is firmly sustained. The first poem announces the theme and shows that the poet, if not writing at his very best, is at least very close to one of his best modes of vision:

> In paths untrodden,
> In the growth by margins of pond-waters,

Escaped from the life that exhibits itself,
From all the standards hitherto publish'd, from the
    pleasures, profits, conformities,
Which too long I was offering to feed my soul,
Clear to me now standards not yet publish'd, clear to
    me that my soul,
That the soul of the man I speak for rejoices in com-
    rades,
Here by myself away from the clank of the world,
Tallying and talk'd to here by tongues aromatic,
No longer abash'd, (for in this secluded spot I can
    respond as I would not dare elsewhere,)
Strong upon me the life that does not exhibit itself, yet
    contains all the rest,
Resolv'd to sing no songs to-day but those of manly
    attachment,
Projecting them along that substantial love,
Afternoon this delicious Ninth-month in my forty-
    first year,
I proceed for all who are or have been young men,
To tell the secret of my nights and days,
To celebrate the need of comrades.

"Scented Herbage of My Breast" is a significant poem because of its poignant use of phallic images and because (if we
read *Leaves of Grass* in the order in which the poems are
printed) it contains Whitman's first extended statement
about the meanings of death. The beginning reader of Whitman might well be suspicious of a poet who writes:

Yet you are beautiful to me, you faint-tinged roots,
    you make me think of death,
Death is beautiful from you, (what indeed is finally
    beautiful except death and love?)

He might suspect that here in the midst of the nineteenth
century there had emerged another vague, sententious and

operatic idea of the beautiful. But happily the idea of death and its relation of love turns out to be one of Whitman's most satisfactory themes. "Song of Myself" would be only a somewhat different poem were not death an undercurrent of its buoyant assertions. But the great poems of the 1858-60 period would be inconceivable without their treatment of death. It is, of course, one of the odd paradoxes of American literature that in the midst of a supposedly vigorous and expanding culture it should have so often found its characteristic accent in meditations upon death. This has been true of such disparate authors as Jonathan Edwards, Poe, Melville, Emily Dickinson, and Hemingway. The salutary tendency of these writers at their best has been to treat death as the occasion of a controlled, sometimes stoic, pathos. This puritan attitude has often redeemed the American imagination just at the point when it might easily have emulated much that is hollow and sententious or merely sentimental in nineteenth-century literature. Although so different from Emily Dickinson, his greatest contemporary among American poets, Whitman resembles her in his sense of how the idea of death may be used in poetry. It is true that both poets could sometimes bathe themselves rather vaguely in mortuary sensations. Yet the stern puritan confrontation of death of which Emily Dickinson was capable is matched in the "Dutch" stubbornness and plain Quaker realism of Whitman. The idea expressed in "Scented Herbage of My Breast" that death may be the "real reality" which is likely at any moment to "dissipate this entire show of appearance" directs our attention to a precarious universe which is a good deal more exciting and eventful than the easy-going world which is a part of Whitman's usual prophetic program. Feelings of this kind round out the character and sharpen the vision of a poet who might otherwise be all too optimistic and superficial. Not merely an exercise in transcendental doctrine but a genuine dread is to be felt in Whitman's sense

Of the terrible doubt of appearances,
Of the uncertainty after all, that we may be deluded,
That may-be reliance and hope are but speculations
  after all,
That may-be identity beyond the grave is a beautiful
  fable only,
May-be the things I perceive, the animals, plants, men,
  hills, shining and flowing waters,
The skies of day and night, colors, densities, forms,
  may-be these are (as doubtless they are) only ap-
  paritions.

In the poems of Emily Dickinson the tragic dilemmas and
anxieties of human life are said to be resolved and placated
by grace of immortality. And this immortality, although conceived in various ways, is often imagined as residing in the
love of "friends." In Whitman, there are none of the ecstatic
or ominous metaphors of Calvinism such as distinguish the
poetry of his contemporary. There is instead a vision of universal progress. Yet the dialectic of the universe involves both
death and life, the temporal and the eternal. And like the
poems of Emily Dickinson the *Calamus* poems tell us that the
love of comrades by some mysterious yet sublime seduction
brings us to a knowledge of death and allows us to perceive
beyond the pale a bright "city of Friends." One need hardly
insist upon the fact that these ideas, as we find them in *Leaves
of Grass*, do not appear as a system and, except for purposes of
exposition, are very little capable of generalization. One is
hardly convinced by Whitman's assertion—taking it as a *philosophical* proposition—that he has examined "the new and
antique, the Greek and Germanic systems" and has discovered that "the base of all metaphysics" is "the dear love of
man for his comrade." One is convinced, rather by the poetic
metaphors with which this idea is concomitant.

> Scented herbage of my breast,
> Leaves from you I glean, I write, to be perused best
>   afterwards,
> Tomb-leaves, body-leaves growing up above me above
>   death,
> Perennial roots, tall leaves, O the winter shall not freeze
>   you delicate leaves.

From the brief lyrics of *Calamus* it is but a step to the richer
orchestrations of "Out of the Cradle Endlessly Rocking."

"Out of the Cradle" is one of Whitman's most considerable
poems. Its pre-eminence is due in part to the poem's well-
known musical form—its intermixture of recitative, aria and
chorus—which allows the poet an unwonted variability of
tonal effects. It is equally due to the closely packed metaphors:

> Out of the cradle endlessly rocking,
> Out of the mocking-bird's throat, the musical shuttle,
> Out of the Ninth-month midnight,
> Over the sterile sands and the fields beyond, where the
>   child leaving his bed wander'd alone, bareheaded,
>   barefoot,
> Down from the shower'd halo,
> Up from the mystic play of shadows twining and twist-
>   ing as if they were alive,
> Out from the patches of briers and blackberries,
> From the memories of the bird that chanted to me,
> From your memories sad brother, from the fitful risings
>   and fallings I heard,
> From under that yellow half-moon late-risen and
>   swollen as if with tears,
> From those beginning notes of yearning and love there
>   in the mist,
> From the thousand responses of my heart never to
>   cease,
> From the myriad thence-arous'd words,
> From the word stronger and more delicious than any,

From such as now they start the scene revisiting,
As a flock, twittering, rising, or overhead passing,
Borne hither, ere all eludes me, hurriedly,
A man, yet by these tears a little boy again,
Throwing myself on the sand, confronting the waves,
I chanter of pains and joys, uniter of here and here-
    after,
Taking all hints to use them, but swiftly leaping be-
    yond them,
A reminiscence sing.

The poetic properties of these lines strike one as being entirely inextricable each from the other, a virtue conspicuously
lacking in Whitman's weaker verses. These lines state the
whole subject matter of the poem. The poem is to be a revisiting of childhood scenes and experiences, and it is to be a
search for the origin of the poet's song, of the "myriad thence-
arous'd words." The poem is not to be an elegy or a dirge for
a lost friend, at least so far as we can learn from the overture.
The meanings of "Out of the Cradle" are suggested by two
earlier titles Whitman gave to it: "A Child's Reminiscence"
and "A Word Out of the Sea."

It is possible, as has often been suggested, that this poem
was written in response to some bereavement in Whitman's
life which may have taken place in or just before 1859. The
"mock bird" calls pathetically for its lost mate and, as the
poet says, "pour'd forth the meanings which I of all men
know." And, as Schyberg has pointed out, one or two passages
in earlier versions of "Out of the Cradle" seem to have a more
personal meaning than they do in the final version. Yet there
are no solid facts upon which to make a specifically biographical interpretation. The bereavement of which Whitman
speaks is clearly that felt by a child, or "a man, yet by these
tears a little boy again." And where it applies neither literally
to the child or symbolically to the bird, it is generalized into

the sense of loss incident to all human life. Nor is it bereavement that the poet is finally talking about. The main subject is the "word" and "Out of the Cradle" is one of those works, like Yeats' "Byzantium" and certain Books of Wordsworth's *Prelude*, which has to be read as a poem about the origin of poetry. It must be observed, however, that Whitman's procedure, like Wordsworth's, is naturalistic, since it traces the roots of imagination to the experiences and psychic dispositions of the poet himself. He does not speak metaphysically of the transformation of experience into symbol as does Yeats. The accent is entirely original.

> The rest might not, but I have treasur'd every note,
> For more than once dimly down to the beach gliding,
> Silent, avoiding the moonbeams, blending myself with
>   the shadows,
> Recalling now the obscure shapes, the echoes, the
>   sounds and sights after their sorts,
> The white arms out in the breakers tirelessly tossing,
> I, with bare feet, a child, the wind wafting my hair,
> Listen'd long and long.

In "Out of the Cradle" Whitman represents the demonic or automatic impulse of poetry by means of the solitary bird—"Demon or bird," he is called. His song is a dirge for the lost mate. But this is merely the literal or narrative occasion of the poem. It is a type of a more general bereavement, a meaning suggested by the image of the maternal sea, the "savage old mother" who is at once so immeasurably attractive and so terrible, who manifests herself as "white arms out in the breakers tirelessly tossing," and as "some old crone rocking the cradle, swathed in sweet garments, bending aside" and incessantly whispering with a "drown'd secret hissing" the "low and delicious word death." The idea of loss is thus converted from water to mother and then generalized, by way of the symbolic connection of mother and sea as well as by the poet's memories of his early love and fear of the sea, to include that inconceivable but sublime sense of loss incident to the emergence of life itself from the all-encompassing waters. In this manner Whitman grasps at the most poignant center of experience, and it is characteristic of him that where other poets would be likely to derive the meaning of life and the origin of imagination from God (or God manifested in nature) and man's relation to Him, Whitman, like Emily Dickinson, derives them from death. Implicit in the work of both poets there is the recognition that death may be taken as the ultimate metaphor of democracy, that only this metaphor can perfectly express the principle of equality; and what was a tragi-comic conceit for Emily Dickinson in those of her poems which play with this idea was for Whitman the lyric mode in which he made his most profound utterances.

As we have observed, Whitman in "Out of the Cradle" is trying to discover where, for him, the poetic power originates. It begins with the first full childhood sense of having irrevocably lost some marvelous and beautiful but also dangerous and threatening person or state of being. It begins with the sense that all life is a mode of death, and flowers with the perception that all imagination is a mode of our sense of death. There can be only one answer to the questions of the boy's soul by the "colloquy" of his early surroundings and experiences. Only one "clue," one "word" can rouse "the tongue's use sleeping" or point out the inevitable path "to the outsetting bard."

> My own songs awaked from that hour;
> And with them the key, the word up from the waves,
> The word of the sweetest song, and all songs,
> That strong and delicious word which, creeping to my
>   feet,

(Or like some old crone rocking the cradle, swathed
    in sweet garments, bending aside,)
The sea whisper'd me.

It all makes an amazingly beautiful composition. If one has
any reservations about the poem, they arise from a sense that
rich as the interweaving of melodic lines is and luxurious as
the imagery is there is sometimes an effect of turgidity. The
poem adequately exists, at any rate, in its simplest terms—the
verbal music, the pathos of the bird, the lilac scent, the boy
on the beach, the white arms in the breakers, the lyric, or
aria, passages that achieve so much unwonted intensity by
being related to but free of the dark subsoil of the poem:

> Shine! shine! shine!
> Pour down your warmth, great sun!
> While we bask, we two together.
>
> Two together!
> Winds blow South, or winds blow North,
> Day come white, or night come black,
> Home, or rivers and mountains from home,
> Singing all time, minding no time,
> While we two keep together.

Although "Out of the Cradle" celebrates the power of imagination to give meanings to chaos and death, another *Sea
Drift* poem, "As I Ebb'd with the Ocean of Life," expresses
the final helplessness of man before the mystery of the universe. The "fierce old mother" appears again in this poem but
she is now more active. That is, the point of view has changed.
Man is no longer a struggling, creative being who has lost
something; he is now a "castaway," a "little wash'd up drift/
A few sands and dead leaves." A walk along the shore at ebb
tide has led the poet to muse on the transiency of life, the
fragility of the resistance to annihilation which the individual
can put up, the instability of organic existence, the evanes-
cence of ideas and "identities." The essence of things is now

discerned in the "sobbing dirge of Nature," and the mystery
of how human life is "out of fathomless workings fermented
and thrown" is contemplated with a dark, lyric pessimism.

The principle of chaos is apparently masculine, an idea, as
has been suggested, which is of some significance in understanding Whitman. In this poem, there appears an image
which is complementary to the maternal sea; Paumonok, the
fish-shaped island, is presented, not in its fish-shape or in any
guise of form or permanence, but as a "friable shore with
trails of débris," as "those slender windrows, / Chaff, straw,
splinters of wood, weeds, and the sea-gluten, / Scum, scales
from shining rocks, leaves of salt-lettuce, left by the tide." It
is a marvelous conception and it reminds us again of how
great a poet Whitman could become under the pressure of his
extraordinary capacity to imagine his own destruction. If
Henry James was justified in claiming for himself "the imagination of disaster," Whitman might with equal justice
claim the sensibility of annihilation. Observing the objects
which symbolize the final infirmity of man in the universe,
Whitman admits the defeat of "this electric self out of the
pride of which I utter poems" and writes these despairing yet
witty lines:

> O baffled, balk'd, bent to the very earth,
> Oppress'd with myself that I have dared to open my
>   mouth,
> Aware now that amid all that blab whose echoes recoil
>   upon me I have not once had the least idea who
>   or what I am,
> But that before all my arrogant poems the real Me
>   stands yet untouch'd, untold, altogether unreach'd
> Withdrawn far, mocking me with mock-congratula
>   tory signs and bows,
> With peals of distant ironical laughter at every word I
>   have written,

Pointing in silence to these songs, and then to the sand
  beneath.

. . . .

Me and mine, loose windrows, little corpses,
Froth, snowy white, and bubbles,
(See, from my dead lips the ooze exuding at last,
See, the prismatic colors glistening and rolling,)
Tufts of straw, sands, fragments,
Buoy'd hither from many moods, one contradicting
  another,
From the storm, the long calm, the darkness, the swell,
Music, pondering, a breath, a briny tear, a dab of liquid
  or soil,
Up just as much out of fathomless workings fermented
  and thrown,
A limp blossom or two, torn, just as much over waves
  floating, drifted at random,
Just as much for us that sobbing dirge of Nature,
Just as much whence we come that blare of the cloud-
  trumpets,
We, capricious, brought hither we know not whence,
  spread out before you,
You up there walking or sitting,
Whoever you are, we too lie in drifts at your feet.

To possess the "sensibility of annihilation" has, as we have
seen, been an ideal of many American writers, from Edwards
and Cooper and Bryant (in his bumbling but impressive
"Thanatopsis") to Stephen Crane, Dreiser, and Hemingway.
In addition to the assertion made above that the "puritan"
moral tone (not doctrine) has been of value to American
writers when they consider death, one may at this point venture a further assertion. The experience and meaning of
death has been well rendered in our literature when the
emotion involved is pathos touched with humor and when it
is evolved (as in the Whitman passage quoted above) by a

particular, even minute, observation. It has been well rendered in works as different as Edwards' "The Flying Spider" (*not* the hell-fire sermon), Bryant's "To a Waterfowl," the poems of Emily Dickinson, Crane's *The Red Badge of Courage*, and James's *The Wings of the Dove*. It has been badly rendered in Melville's *Pierre* (*Moby Dick* may be left out of this discussion as a grand exception) and in the naturalistic novel from Norris to Dreiser because it is so often the case that the pity evoked by the writer is self-pity and the universe depicted is abstractly observed and heavily portentous with a vulgar ideology—all too resonant with the "blare of the cloud-trumpets" Whitman for a perilous moment hears. There is no self-pity in Whitman's poem; the "sobbing dirge" is "of Nature"; these are the tears of things. Portentous abstractions and romantic nihilism are great temptations to the American mind when it dwells on the idea of death. Death arouses in us a desire to philosophize about free will and determinism, to posit a universe in the image of our muddy cogitations and our hypostatized self-pity—see, for example, the moving but finally inferior death scene in Dreiser's *American Tragedy* with its many echoes of Whitman. This is, of course, not natural or inevitable; it is backward and eccentric if our standard is the representation of death in the *Iliad*, the *Aeneid* or *Hamlet*. If Whitman may justly claim in this matter to escape our backwardness, surely one reason is that he has taken his own measure—seen himself and made us see him—by means of the "laughter" and the "mock-congratulatory signs and bows" of that exquisite ironist he calls "the real Me." In a poem about death and nature the healthy presence of this ironist is a sign of greatness. It helps to make "As I Ebb'd with Ocean of Life" a great elegy of the self and to explain why one feels that Whitman's "friable shore with trails of débris," his "slender windrows," are unsurpassed as elegiac images.

CHAPTER IV

THE CIVIL WAR AND AFTER

APRIL 12, 1861, was as important a date in the life of Walt Whitman as it was in the history of the United States. Sauntering down Broadway after attending an opera on that evening, he heard the newsboys proclaiming the attack on Fort Sumter, and he stepped into the lighted lobby of the Metropolitan Hotel to read the reports. Whitman soon sensed that this must be a critical time not only for the nation but for the patriot-prophet who had undertaken to celebrate its virtues and to mend its faults. The prophetic Whitman had been in abeyance during the bad times just before the war while the nation stood divided, confused, and disillusioned and the poet, having little heart for moral exhortation, examined the private sources of his being and of his poetry and came near to the conclusion that his "identity" might already be running out into the sands and so to its annihilation. But now regeneration and a new life seemed possible to Walt Whitman. So we might gather from his somewhat quaint resolution of April 18 henceforth to live clean and drink nothing but water and pure milk. And so we sense from the excited energy and the feeling of spiritual liberation in the hasty but vigorous martial verses he wrote in 1861, and later included in *Drum Taps*.

Yet, as we have observed before, the heavy inertia of Whitman's personality did not allow sudden mutations. And accordingly it should not surprise us that not until late in 1862 did Walt forsake his usual mode of life. He did not enlist as a soldier, a fact that was later to call forth the charge, from Thomas Wentworth Higginson and other unfriendly critics, that he had been a slacker. Apparently Whitman suffered no anguish, such as a later admirer of his, Henry James, seems to have felt, over his disinclination to enlist. There were good reasons. He might fall back on his genuine streak of Quaker mildness, even though he had written such warlike editorials at the time of the Mexican War. More persuasive, however, was the fact that after his brother George's early enlistment, Walt was virtually the head of the family. Perhaps also, now that his spirits were beginning to revive and his earnest feeling for his country was having a new birth, he might justifiably claim that his duty was to write about the war rather than fight in it.

But it was to be some time before he could respond to the war as a great writer. Meanwhile, he continued with journalism, turning out in 1861 and 1862 a series of twenty-five historical sketches of Brooklyn for a Brooklyn newspaper. More significantly, he continued his practice of the last year or two of regularly visiting, at the New York Hospital, the sick and injured stage drivers whom he had come so engagingly to idealize—riding up and down Broadway, like a boy, beside the drivers on their high seats and admiring their professional competence and listening to their talk. In later years a doctor at the hospital remembered the large, bland, grizzled visitor, neatly dressed in blue flannel coat, baggy gray trousers, and woolen shirt opened at the neck, who sometimes talked about literature with the doctors but would never discuss himself. Whitman was sometimes seen at Pfaff's drinking beer with the doctors, doubtless *before* his resolution to take only water and milk, and before, also, the dramatic occasion in 1861 when he walked out of Pfaff's never to return again (except for a brief visit twenty years later), having gotten into a fight between Unionists and Copperheads and having had his hair pulled in a scuffle with a partisan of the South. Before his journey to the front at the end of 1862, there were more of the habitual rambles about the countryside of Long Island, including a visit to his sister Mary at Greenport and an idyllic chance meeting with a sloop full of junketing young people who took him aboard and sailed to Montauk Point.

On December 13, 1862, George Whitman, a captain in the 51st New York Volunteers, was wounded at Fredericksburg. Walt left for the front immediately, arriving at Falmouth, Virginia, on December 19. Although he found that his brother was out of danger and did not need him, Whitman spent the rest of the month, as he recalled in *Speciman Days*, helping the sick and wounded and in January accompanied a group of invalided soldiers to Washington. Here he decided not to go home but to devote himself to the care of the soldiers. And so he found himself embarked on the career of hospital visiting which was to occupy him for the next three or four years. The adoption of his new personality in these years —the "wound dresser," the nursing father—was, of course, one of the exemplary acts of Whitman's life and indeed of American history. By the end of 1864 Whitman estimated that he had made six hundred visits to the hospitals and seen "eighty thousand to one hundred thousand of the wounded and sick." There was a certain mysticism but, whatever its emotional sources, a total genuineness, in Whitman's feeling for his new career. "I believe," he wrote in an article for *The New York Times*, "that even the moving around among the men, or through the ward, of a hearty, healthy, clean, strong, generous-souled person, man or woman, full of humanity and love, sending out invisible, constant currents thereof, does immense good to the sick and wounded." An untold number of the wounded had good reason to be grateful to Whitman— those who called out after the large gray man who passed through the wards with his knapsack full of candy, oranges, tobacco, writing paper, and stamps, "Walt, Walt, Walt, come again! come again!" and those who, dying, heard themselves called "my dear" and felt Whitman's fatherly kiss. Henry James was to commemorate what he believed to be a shared experience by remembering, in his *Notes of a Son and Brother*, that his own visits to the convalescent troops in Rhode Island during the war had been paralleled by "dear old Walt"; and by adding that "I like to treat myself to making out that I can scarce have brought to the occasion . . . less of the consecrating sentiment than he."

Outside the hospitals Whitman led his usual desultory life, commonly rising late, eating two meals a day, getting through his daily work in the Paymaster's Office or the Department of the Interior in a few hours, and then ambling slowly back to the hospitals. A circle of literary admirers gradually formed about him, including Eldridge, his bankrupt Boston publisher, John Burroughs, like Eldridge a government clerk, and William O'Connor, a young man of literary aspirations who was to be Whitman's most fiery and contentious apologist. For the first time Whitman became the idol of a coherent body of followers, all of whom felt the extraordinary "personal magnetism" of their prophet and all of whom believed that he was something genuinely new in the world, an American miracle, possibly a divine intercessor in the affairs of men. The all-or-nothing attitude expressed by Burroughs seems accurately to reflect the mentality of the Whitman disciples, both the Washington group and those who later gathered around him at Camden: "He is, in my opinion," wrote Burroughs, "either more and different from any other poet, or he is a ridiculous failure. I am fully persuaded that he belongs to an entirely new class of geniuses which has no type in the past; and that he is justified and explained on entirely new grounds." Gratifying as this adulation was, the influence of the disciples was in the long run a bad one. The disciples admired Whitman's program and misunderstood or ignored his poetry, and theirs was one of the powerful influences which made of Whitman a self-publicist and self-parodist, and gradually isolated him from everything in the world which did not seem to accord with their *Leaves-of-Grass* cult.

By 1868 Whitman was making an impression for the first time in Europe. Young poets and critics in England were taking him up. William Rossetti published a selection called *Poems of Walt Whitman,* and other pre-Raphaelites, including Swinburne, were attracted to the American poet of democracy, in whom they saw a companion to another of their heroes, William Blake. Whitman's name was soon known in Germany and France, and by the early 1870's in Denmark. Whitman had also become famous among the inhabitants of Washington, not as a poet, but as a figure. During the war, Lincoln had been aware of him and the two had nodded in the streets. In later years, young women rose to give him their seats in the horsecars, inscribed photographs were on sale in the stores, and passers-by hailed him as "Walt."

Outwardly Whitman's fortunes appeared to be immensely improving. With the assistance of the poet himself, O'Connor and Burroughs had launched by 1866 a campaign to popularize and justify their prophet by means of reviews, articles, and biographies. By the fall of 1863 Walt believed himself to be recovered from the dark mood of a few years before. If in 1860 he had published poems, such as "So Long," which intimated that his career might be at an end, in 1863 he wrote with a renewed assurance that the work of his life was "making poems": "I *must* be continually bringing out poems—now is the heyday—I shall range along the high plateau of my life and capacity for a few years now, and then swiftly descend." Whitman's feelings about his career remained sanguine in 1865 when he published *Drum Taps,* adding to it, after Lincoln's death, a sequel which included "When Lilacs Last in the Dooryard Bloom'd." He thought *Drum Taps* superior to anything he had written, "certainly more perfect as a work of art." In 1867 he brought out the fourth edition of *Leaves of Grass*, which although it exhibits no new poems of any significance, was the product of very extensive attempts at editing and rearranging. He was also able to bring out a fifth edition in 1871-2, which included so auspicious a new poem as "Passage to India."

Yet despite this activity and despite the fact that Whitman thought himself to be ranging along the high plateau of his literary career, the truth is that, as a poet, he was already on the downgrade. The inspired lyricist of 1855 and 1859 was becoming less a lyricist and more an editor, a publicist, and even an imitator of his own works, just as the demonic prophet was becoming more and more the bland and self-conventionalized and somewhat fuzzy-minded sage. With the exception of "When Lilacs Last in the Dooryard Bloom'd" and one or two of the *Drum Taps* poems, Whitman's verse shows that during and after the war he was living on his literary capital. Changes in his poetic accent and in his ideas are observable, but these are on the whole redeployments of emphasis and refinements of style.

Whitman nowhere tells us what he meant by saying that he regarded the *Drum Taps* poems as artistically superior to anything he had hitherto done. Taken as a group they surely do not live up to the poet's high opinion of them. But they do suggest what he may have had in mind when he spoke of their artistic quality, or if they are not better than his previous work, they try for somewhat different effects. Whitman seems consciously to have striven for a more taut and often a more conventional versification, a less luxurious verbal texture, and a sharper, more realistic imagery. The poems are best when they are strictly and sharply "imagistic" and when they efficiently compromise between the larger, looser oratorical effect and conventional meters, for, as must be plain to every reader, Whitman cannot approach too closely to conventional meter without becoming (as in "O Captain, My Captain" and even in "Pioneers! O Pioneers!"—both poems of this period) not so much conventional as merely mechanical.

The new realism visible in *Drum Taps* seems to be a result of the emergence Whitman had been able to make, under the pressure of the excitement about the war, from the introspective, ruminating mood of the late 1850's. A similar "return" from a period of "withdrawal" had taken place in 1841, when he was able to make a decisive new connection with experience by returning, from his desultory rustication and random employment on Long Island, to the panoramic reality of New York. Another one of these newly made connections with reality is chronicled in those sections of *Specimen Days* which exhibit a minute and tenacious exploration of nature which, one would conclude, helped Whitman to recover from the disorganized state of mind induced by his first paralytic shock. This pattern of alternating regression and thrusts outward to reality must be understood before any general account of Whitman's literary realism can be given. It indicates, for example, how strong were Whitman's personal impulses away from reality, reinforced, as these impulses always were, by his tendency toward Quaker mysticism and transcendental idealism. It suggests a perpetual internal war in Whitman which is not in accord with the view that the poet arrived at his characteristic attitudes by way of mere psychic laxity and sensuous passivity. And this alternating pattern suggests, too, how one may account for the varying qualities of the poet's realism. By observing the particular impulses behind the return from this or that particular withdrawal, one gains a point of view toward, let us say, the omnivorous undifferentiating realism of the 1840's, the transcendentalist or organic realism of

"Song of Myself" (after the withdrawal of the early 1850's), the fragmented, imagistic realism of *Drum Taps*, the plain stubborn factuality of the best passages in *Specimen Days*.

Probably the reader who knew a great deal of Whitman but had never happened to read one of the best and most famous of the *Drum Taps* poems—"Cavalry Crossing a Ford"—would identify it as Whitman's. Yet from the unusually laconic title to the last word, the poem is something new in the Whitman canon:

> A line in long array where they wind betwixt green
>   islands,
> They take a serpentine course, their arms flash in the
>   sun—hark to the musical clank,
> Behold the silvery river, in it the splashing horses loiter-
>   ing stop to drink,
> Behold the brown-faced men, each group, each person
>   a picture, the negligent rest on the saddles,
> Some emerge on the opposite bank, others are just
>   entering the ford—while
> Scarlet and blue and snowy white,
> The guidon flags flutter gayly in the wind.

But aside from "Cavalry Crossing a Ford" and one or two similar pieces, such as "An Army Corps on the March," the more martial of the *Drum Taps* poems are of little interest. They illustrate, however, the poet's state of mind after the firing on Fort Sumter. He greets the war as a tonic and a moral imperative—"My limbs, my veins dilate, my theme is clear at last." This is the time for idealistic commitment, as he says, and all merely prudential considerations must be put aside. It is a time for release, for adventure, for eagles, drums, marching feet, and music. It is a time, as we read in "Long, Too Long America," for the nation to rise from its ease and its lethargy and pass through the trial by fire which will prove its final worth. And it is a time, of course, for new American bards, who will put in abeyance the "pale [but unimaginable] poetling seated at a desk lisping cadenzas piano."

Another group of the *Drum Taps* poems is made up of meditative and elegiac pieces such as "The Wound-Dresser." As Whitman says in this poem (although the lines were inserted in 1881):

> Arous'd and angry, I'd thought to beat the alarum,
>   and urge relentless war,
> But soon my fingers fail'd me, my face droop'd and
>   I resign'd myself,
> To sit by the wounded and soothe them, or silently
>   watch the dead.

The best of these meditative poems are the beautiful "Reconciliation," "Dirge for Two Veterans," and "As I Lay with My Head in Your Lap, Camerado." Yet good as these are, they do not live up to Whitman's apparent expectations of them. And indeed it is the sad fact that Whitman's war experiences did not find a satisfactory expression in his poetry, although some of them did in *Specimen Days*. Whitman's statement in "A Backward Glance O'er Travel'd Roads" that without the three or four years of the Civil War "and the experiences they gave, *Leaves of Grass* would not now be existing" is simply not true, although it does indicate how serious a crisis in his life Whitman took these years to be. The truth is that Whitman's career of hospital visiting became a substitute for poetry and not the inspiration of it.

The main weakness of the Civil War poems arises from the poet's using them too personally, to work out troubles of his own. This is why so many of the stirring, martial pieces seem not only stirring but hysterical.

Henry James's youthful review of *Drum Taps* was unfair and supercilious and showed none of his later appreciation of Whitman, but he was perceptive in pointing out "the pro-

longed muscular strain" the poems seemed to exert in order
to soar, and the sense Whitman gave, in writing about the
war, of his affinity with "minds which are bullied by the
accidents of the affair." And indeed there is a great deal of
strained and flustered overexcitement in such a line as "Proud
and passionate city—mettlesome, mad, extravagant city!"

Melville's amateurish "Battle Pieces" are superior to the
Drum Taps group, even though in three or four poems Whitman displays a power of organizing images in a pure lyric
mode which was beyond Melville. One has only to compare
Whitman's "Pensive on Her Dead Gazing," the subject of
which is the healing, reconciling power of nature, with any of
Melville's poems on the same topic, to see that Melville is able
to find metaphors profoundly involved in nature and history,
whereas Whitman (although there are good lines in "Pensive
on Her Dead Gazing") is by comparison vague, pantheistic,
and hortatory.

One is inclined to see in *Drum Taps,* as was suggested above,
a critical juncture in Whitman's development. These poems
have all the signs of having been written by a poet whose
visionary grasp of things is weakening. The plastic power
which since 1855 had been able at least intermittently to unite
an extraordinary capacity for realistic observation and for
experience with an equally strong capacity for adducing vital
emblematic or mythic abstractions so that the whole was
transmuted into an "organic" vision can no longer enforce the
union with its old assurance, and except on rare occasions, will
not be able to do so again. The elements of the vision fall
apart, so that we are left with a simple (though sometimes
interesting) realism on the one hand and on the other that
vague and lifeless universalization of feelings which we find
in much of Whitman's later verse. In *Drum Taps* we have an
example of the break-up of the old-fashioned transcendentalist "organic" sensibility which before the Civil War offered its

various ways of imaginatively associating the real with the ideal, the burgeoning concretion of American life with the large abstractions it encouraged. We should hardly expect Walt Whitman to find any massive solution to this radical crisis of sensibility. Implicitly his crisis of the imagination was that of American literature generally. We should hardly expect him to undertake the reconstitution of a unified sensibility from the operational base of realism, which has been the task of our literature since the Civil War. He could but lament the Civil War, which was not only a war between the states but a war which had broken out within the poetic imagination. His poem called "Reconciliation" longs not only for a re-established peace but for a poetic or mythic "word":

> Word over all, beautiful as the sky,
> Beautiful that war and all its deeds of carnage must in
>   time be utterly lost,
> That the hands of the sisters Death and Night inces-
>   santly softly wash again, and ever again, this soil'd
>   world;
> For my enemy is dead, a man divine as myself is dead,
> I look where he lies white-faced and still in the coffin—
>   I draw near,
> Bend down and touch lightly with my lips the white
>   face in the coffin.

There remained for Whitman, however, the writing of one more great poem. Apparently stemming from the mood of "Out of the Cradle," "When Lilacs Last in the Dooryard Bloom'd" is also related to "Crossing Brooklyn Ferry," capturing, as it does, the richness of the former and the vital abstractness and serene austerity of the latter. In the unique beauty of the Lincoln elegy one perceives both a farewell to poetry and the dim lineaments of a possible "late manner."

Lincoln had, of course, meant much to Whitman. He had

voted for Lincoln in 1860 and had seen the President-elect when he stopped at the Astor House in New York on his way to Washington. Whitman noted how Lincoln "looked with curiosity" at the sullen, silent crowd that had gathered to see him, how he uttered no word but merely stretched his long limbs and stood there, an "uncouth" figure in his black suit and tall hat, gazing at the crowd with "perfect composure and coolness." Whitman thought he saw in Lincoln's posture "a dash of comedy, almost of farce, such as Shakespeare puts in his blackest tragedies," a description so accurate that one might imagine Lincoln unconsciously to describe himself in the same manner.

Matthiessen has pointed out the relevance of the Lincoln lecture Whitman was accustomed to give in later years to one's understanding of the genesis of the elegy. In this lecture Whitman recalled seeing the President on the occasion of the second inaugural address and noting how deeply cut were the marks of fatigue and worry on the "dark brown face" which still showed, however, "all the old goodness, tenderness, sadness, and canny shrewdness." Whitman recalled that just before the President stepped forth to the portico of the Capitol, the violent storm of the morning ceased and the day became so preternaturally clear that in the afternoon the stars shown "long, long before they were due." He recalled, too, the dramatic changes of weather in the weeks preceding the inauguration and how superbly beautiful some of the nights had been in the intervals of fair weather. Especially beautiful was the star he was to use with such effect in the elegy—"The western star, Venus, in the earlier hours of evening, has never been so large, so clear; it seems as if it told something, as if it held rapport indulgent with humanity, with us Americans."

It is of some psychological interest that when Whitman learned of the assassination, he was with his mother in Brooklyn. He described the scene in *Specimen Days:* "The day of the murder we heard the news very early in the morning. Mother prepared breakfast—and other meals afterward—as usual; but not a mouthful was eaten all day by either of us. We each drank half a cup of coffee; that was all. Little was said. We got every newspaper morning and evening, and the frequent extras of that period, and pass'd them silently to each other." The mood of hushed consecration in Whitman's poem, its treatment of death as a providential mother or bride, the large part played in the poem by reminiscences of childhood, such as the singing bird, the lilac that once bloomed in the dooryard of the Whitman farm—all these elements might have entered into the poem in any case but they are doubtless more of the poem's essence because of the circumstances under which Whitman first reflected upon the death of the President. (It is of some interest, too, that in *Specimen Days* Whitman described the star by which he symbolizes Lincoln as "maternal"; he had watched the setting of Venus on the night on March 18, 1879 and had jotted down the following: "Venus nearly down in the west, of a size and lustre as if trying to outshow herself, before departing. Teeming, maternal orb—I take you again to myself. I am reminded of that spring preceding Abraham Lincoln's murder, when I, restlessly haunting the Potomac banks, around Washington city, watch'd you, off there, aloof, moody as myself.")

The feelings expressed in this poem are exceedingly personal and exceedingly abstract. The death of the great person stirs the poet not to a tragic sense of life but to its exquisite pathos. The idea of redemption and eternal life is present, but the mood is aesthetic and moral rather than religious. In these qualities, as in its rather theatrical decor, Whitman's poem is closer in spirit to *The Wings of the Dove* than to the classic elegy.

If we compare "When Lilacs Last in the Dooryard Bloom'd" with "Lycidas," the greatest of English elegies, certainly notable differences emerge. "Lycidas" is, of course, written in the pastoral tradition, the convention of which is that a society of shepherds and more or less mythical personages mourns for the loss of a fellow shepherd. Nature, or its presiding geniuses, is chidden for its cruelty but joins in the universal mourning. And the consolatory thought is expressed that the dead person has actually escaped death and is assured of immortality. Whitman's democratic elegy departs from the practice of Milton exactly as we might expect. There is no society of shepherds in Whitman's poem; there is no image of any society at all, except of the sketchiest kind—on the one hand there are brief concrete images of "separate houses" with their "daily usages" and little groups of somber citizens at the depots watching the coffin, and, on the other hand, a generalized sense of the whole nation in mourning. Lincoln himself is absent from the poem, there being hardly a trace of either his person or his personality until the very end of the poem, where Whitman speaks vaguely of "the sweetest, wisest soul of all my days and lands." By comparison we are told a good deal in "Lycidas" about Edward King, his youthful accomplishments and the promise of his career; and we are made very poignantly to feel the loneliness of the unfortunate youth as his body is tossed by the whelming tide. Whitman had formed sharp impressions of the powerful individuality of Lincoln, as we know from his graphic remarks about him elsewhere. He had even complained, in *Specimen Days*, that none of the portraits he had seen had at all caught the essential qualities of Lincoln's face, "the peculiar color, the lines of it, the eyes, mouth, expression." So that the impersonality of his elegy is all the more strongly brought home to us when Whitman writes:

> Here, coffin that slowly passes,
> I give you my sprig of lilac,

and we realize that not only has the poet not thought directly
of the man in the coffin but that he has moved immediately
into the abstract and universal, for he adds:

> Nor for you, for one alone,
> Blossoms and branches green to coffins all I bring,
> For fresh as the morning, thus would I chant a song
>   for you O sane and sacred death.

Whitman's unacknowledged convention, here as everywhere,
makes it impossible for him to conceive either the being or
the value of the individual without conceiving him as an example of mankind in general. Were he to read Whitman's
poem, Milton would doubtless observe that instead of bestow-
ing flowers upon Lincoln, as he should, the poet bestows them
first on all the dead equally and then on death itself.

Elegiac feeling in American literature does not, in fact,
characteristically take for its occasion the death of an individual—a Bion, an Edward King, a Keats, a Wellington. Or if it
does, as in Whitman's poem, it moves quickly away from the
particularity of the occasion, and without proposing the dead
person as an example of tragic crisis in the human spirit or in
human history. The American elegiac sensibility—in Cooper,
Melville, Thoreau, Mark Twain, James, and others—is most
strongly engaged by the sense of lost modes of innocence, lost
possibilities of brotherhood, magnanimity, and freedom, lost
sources of moral spontaneity and spiritual refreshment. The
tone is of pathos, nostalgia, and despair. The emotions come
to rest, if at all, in the personal virtues of forebearance and
resignation—not in metaphysical, religious, or political orders
of meaning. There is kinship in Cooper's lament for Lake
Glimmerglass, Mark Twain's musings over Huck Finn and
Jim on their raft, Isabel Archer's cry, "Oh my Brother," at the
death of Ralph Touchett, and Walt Whitman's plea to his
dim, evanescent "companions" in the Lincoln poem.

To set off the large abstractions of the Lincoln elegy there is really only one individual in the poem, the poet himself. To be sure, in "Lycidas" the poet makes his personal grief, his personal presence, and his own aspirations strongly felt; yet he finds solace for his grief and an enhanced understanding of his own probable fate by representing a society of actual and mythical persons who also grieve, and by showing the profound involvement of the dead man, and thus of himself and of all men, in the alternately destructive and healing motions of nature in a divinely directed order. In Whitman's poem the poet finds solace for his grief, not by placing himself in a grieving society but by withdrawing from the world and, in effect, curing his grief by feeling the more powerful emotion of loneliness. And the poem then recounts the poet's search for comrades, whom he finds in the symbolic star and singing bird and finally in death itself. There is no doubt that something morally incomplete has taken place when a poet is unable to speak of the death of a man—and he a beloved man— except in terms of his own loneliness. Yet there can be no doubt about the surpassing beauty of the verse:

> Then with the knowledge of death as walking one
>   side of me,
> And the thought of death close-walking the other side
>   of me,
> And I in the middle as with companions, and as holding
>   the hands of companions,
> I fled forth to the hiding receiving night that talks not,
> Down to the shores of the water, the path by the
>   swamp in the dimness,
> To the solemn shadowy cedars and ghostly pines so
>   still.

If the poet of "When Lilacs Last in the Dooryard Bloom'd" does not place himself in any ostensible society, neither does he very profoundly place himself in nature. Had he read

Moby Dick, Tocqueville might have found an exception to his prediction that American writers, though they might be profoundly moved by the majestic spectacle of mankind, would not attempt to grasp the deeper implications of man's involvement in nature. But like much of Whitman's poetry, the Lincoln elegy bears out this prediction. Whitman is entirely incapable of conceiving anything like Milton's image of Lycidas, who "visit'st the bottom of the monstrous world." In contrast to Milton's tragic conception of nature, Whitman's grasp upon nature issues, not in a vision of universal order (or disorder), but either in the affective pathos of somewhat theatrical symbols like the lilac and the cedars and pines or in the brooding, lyric but abstract meditations upon death.

It must be noted finally that in contrast to that in "Lycidas" the feeling of immortality is extremely weak in Whitman's poem. There is no liberating promise of personal immortality to the dead man, and at the end we find a beautiful but very sad recessional instead of the buoyant promise of "fresh fields, and pastures new." The symbol of the lilac "blooming, returning with spring" recurs, with its suggestion of resurrection. But this does not at all succeed in releasing the poet from his conviction that he has found the ultimate felicity of comradeship in the equalitarian democracy of death itself.

What we do supremely have in the Lincoln elegy is the expression of Whitman's native elegance and refinement. These are not qualities which we usually assign to this poet. When T. S. Eliot referred to that excessive American refinement which did not belong to civilization but was already beyond it, he was thinking of the refinement of Boston. He might have added the conventional opinion that Whitman well represents the opposite strain of American life. But as we have noted before, Whitman is in some ways an extremely sophisticated, even a decadent poet. There is a premature old age in his poetry, as there was in the man himself. His elegiac utterances sound an unmistakable note of Virgilian weariness. And if the mind whose imprint we read on the Lincoln elegy is harmonious and moving, it is also in danger of an excessive refinement. It is in danger of wishing to substitute antiseptics for the healing processes of nature in which it cannot quite believe any more. How else is one to account for the sterile, the really Egyptian, atmosphere of odors, perfumes, herbage, pine, and cedar, to say nothing of the outright lyric worship of death itself?

Yet despite its artificiality "When Lilacs Last in the Door-yard Bloom'd" stands up well if we compare it with other expressions of the refined American spirit—the "Sunday Morning" of Wallace Stevens, let us say, and James's *The Wings of the Dove* and *The Golden Bowl,* and Eliot's *Four Quartets.* Different as these works are they share a tendency toward the abstract forms of myth and music, allegations of portents and miracles, appeals to the restorative cosmic forces. It is a "late" work, and (within the Whitman canon) it has the sound, as well as the emotional appeal, of a swan song.

The spirit and meaning of the poems Whitman wrote in the 1870's might be summed up by the following:

> Joy, shipmate, joy!
> (Pleas'd to my soul at death I cry,)
> Our life is closed, our life begins,
> The long, long anchorage we leave,
> The ship is clear at last, she leaps!
> She swiftly courses from the shore,
> Joy, shipmate, joy!

Whitman's great meditative poems had led him, by the time he came to write his Lincoln elegy, to state that death was a terminus, and a good in itself. He now set about denying this, and the characteristic assertion of his later poems is that after death the soul sails outward on its hopeful voyage to a blissful shore, just as, after the Civil War, America with its science, its expanding industry and railroads, its healthy progressive spirit also sets out on a hopeful voyage (or is reborn by a divinely ordained parturition, as the poet is likely to say in a metaphor only less common than that of the ship). It is hard to know where the ship is bound for, except that it is transporting mankind toward a happy realm variously identified as eternity and universal democracy. Of course, Whitman had been expressing this vision of the future from the very beginning; it found its first full expression in "Salut au Monde" (1856), and this poem has consequently been taken as an important advance beyond "Song of Myself." The poem has, to be sure, a certain charm—the charm of the benevolent American spirit confidently extending the hand of democratic friendship to the races of the world—the "Brazilian vaquero," the "real Parisian," the "thoughtful Armenian," the "Hottentot with clicking palate" (and as we later learned to say, "with his quart of milk"). Yet an abundance of absurd questions nag the reader. Why, for example, is the Armenian "thoughtful," whereas the Spaniard is merely Spanish? It has often been said that this poem shows a growing ability to reach beyond the limits of "Song of Myself" toward the universal scope and lyric power of the poet's later manner—the touchstone of the later manner being, perhaps, "Passage to India." But this idea seems to be the product of an unexamined academic belief in progress, according to which poets improve with age and with the acquisition of "ideas." The shifting quality of Whitman's verse makes one think that whenever he was headed for the universal he was headed for trouble. It seems to be one of our American assumptions that there is something inherently good and beautiful about the universal. Yet all too often when we praise a poem for having universal significance we mean no more than that it has divested itself of troublesome and recalcitrant particularity and dissipated its energies into this or that general idea which is more readily available to critical or moralistic discussion than are the other elements of poetry.

If pieces like "Passage to India" (1868), and "Song of the Universal" (1874), together with the large number of related poems, do not appeal to us very much, it is because Whitman has given up poetry and become a speechmaker. This seems clearly illustrated by the following three lines from "Passage to India":

> The Past—the dark unfathom'd retrospect!
> The teeming gulf—the sleepers and the shadows!
> The past—the infinite greatness of the past!

After an excellent (if derivative) first line, and a satisfactory second, the poet is tongue-tied and the orator takes over, declaiming vulgarly from his editorial chair or his public platform.

Toward the end of this poem Whitman exclaims:

> O sun and moon and all you stars! Sirius and Jupiter!
> Passage to you!
>
> Passage, immediate passage! the blood burns in my
> veins!
> Away O soul! hoist instantly the anchor!
> Cut the hawsers—haul out—shake out every sail!
> Have we not stood here like trees in the ground long
> enough?
> Have we not grovel'd here long enough, eating and
> drinking like mere brutes?
> Have we not darken'd and dazed ourselves with books
> long enough?

The trouble here is that the answer is so insistent: No, not if the alternative is a merely vague spirituality, a hollow optimism, a sententious courting of immortality, a mystic identification with the universe. Melville's comment on Goethe, in a letter to Hawthorne, might apply as well to Whitman. "In reading some of Goethe's sayings, so worshiped by his votaries, I come across this, *Live in the All.* That is to say, your separate identity is but a wretched one,—good; but get out of yourself, spread and expand yourself, and bring to yourself the tinglings of life that are felt in the flowers and the woods, that are felt in the planets Saturn and Venus, and the Fixed Stars. What nonsense! Here is a fellow with a raging toothache. My dear boy, Goethe says to him, you are sorely afflicted with that tooth; but you must *live in the all*, and then you will be happy! As with all great genius, there is an immense deal of flummery in Goethe."

Whitman's later poetry* bespeaks a mind in which productive tensions have been relaxed, conflicts dissipated, particulars generalized, inequities equalized. Whitman had lost his intuition of what in *Democratic Vistas* he cogently described as those "developments either in Nature or human personality in which power (dearest of all to the sense of the artist), transacts itself." The musing, humorous, paradoxically indolent but unpredictably energetic satyr-poet of the early 1850's becomes the large, bland, gray personage with the vague, light blue eyes and the circumambient beard. Dionysius becomes not Apollonian but positively Hellenistic —prematurely old, nerveless, soothsaying, spiritually universalized. The deft and flexible wit disappears along with the contraries and disparities which once produced it. The pa-

---

* Certain of Whitman's later poems have valuable qualities which I shall, however, not attempt to single out. I shall content myself with simply naming those poems which in any account of Whitman's work should not go unmentioned. These include "Tears," "A Noiseless, Patient Spider" (1862), "The Base of All Metaphysics," "Song of the Exposition," "Song of the Redwood Tree," "On the Beach, at Night," "Sparkles from the Wheel," "Prayer of Columbus," and "The Dalliance of Eagles."

thos, once so moving when the poet contemplated the
disintegration of the self or felt the loss which all living things
know, is now generalized out into a vague perception of the
universal. The ocean, which in "Out of the Cradle Endlessly
Rocking" is felt as the source of being and is said to be paradoxically fearful and infinitely delightful, is, in the later
poems, merely a featureless and homogeneous medium in
which the soul seeks its perfect equalization with all things.

After the Civil War, Whitman had lost his quite extraordinary ability to behold the self of which he speaks in "Song
of Myself" with the awe-struck excitement of one who has
confronted an uncanny and preternatural presence; in short,
he had lost his feeling for the self as "Walt Whitman, a
kosmos, of Manhattan the son" or as that mysterious being of
whom he asks, "Who goes there? hankering, gross, mystical,
nude," or as the ironical "real Me" with his courtly, mocking bows. These images of the self owed a good deal of their
energy and drama to the poet's illusion of being able to take
onto himself the vivid power of a lusty young nation and a
vigorous, progressive universe. To have an "identity" was to
be a discrete being, a "simple separate person," and at the
same time one with the "En-masse." By 1859 this paradox of
identity had lost its tension and broken down, in both its
terms. That is, Whitman's personal troubles and doubts led
him to question whether the self really had any dependable
psychological or metaphysical status at all, and at the same
time the confusion and aimlessness of a nation on the brink
of the war gave little assurance that it would continue to be
a source of strength and an object of admiration. The war was
Whitman's salvation as a man, but his doom as a poet. America, redeeming and cleansing itself in the war, was once again
a powerful and admirable spectacle. But the self could no
longer be reinstated as an independent power in dialectic in-
teraction with the en-masse, for whereas it once vigorously

appropriated the power of the nation and yet sustained itself in opposition, it now increasingly surrendered its independent status and projected itself onto the nation and the "universal." The first term in the paradox of identity capitulated to the second: the simple, separate person could now apprehend itself only as it merged with the en-masse. The brash, egotistic Whitman and the frightened, doubting Whitman both give way to the self-sacrificing, even self-annihilating hospital visitor.

Whitman himself was aware, in a sense, of the shift of ground he was making. In a review of his own poem called "As a Strong Bird on Pinions Free" (later called "Thou Mother with Thy Equal Brood") he wrote, in 1872, that so far the *Leaves* had expressed "a great composite Democratic individual" but that now the poet (a "plain unsuspected old customer, dressed in gray and wearing no necktie") inaugurates "a great composite Democratic nationality." Whitman seems at this time to have thought of starting a new book built around such poems as "Passage to India" which would be distinguished from the *Leaves* proper, as he said elsewhere, by its "thread-voice, more or less audible, of an aggregate, inseparable, unprecedented, vast, composite, electric *Democratic Nationality*." Clearly Whitman's intention to celebrate "nationality" did not imply that he wished to write only as a nationalist. America was in the later poems democracy in general; it was the archetype of an ideal equalitarian planet and cosmos—a federated One World with mystic or occult sanctions. The individual, ideally, was the citizen of the cosmos, finding his reality and destiny, as John Kinnaird has written, "in his universalizing commitments."

Idiosyncratic as it is, Whitman's turn of mind as we see it in the later poems shares a tendency toward the ultimate, the abstract, and the occult which was clearly visible in other American writers of the time. If, for example, we were to compare Whitman's "Song of the Exposition" (1871) with Henry Adams's chapter (in the *Education*) on the Chicago Exposition of 1893, we might reasonably speculate that Whitman's optimism and Adams' pessimism are opposite sides of the same coin. Both writers tend to conceive of the American destiny in purely abstract and even occult terms, Adams picturing a fearful collision of alleged "forces," Whitman picturing a beautiful but vague harmony of forces. Both writers exhibit, in this aspect of their work, what might be called the higher crankishness. Yet both Whitman and Adams were following the general tendency of our writers at the end of the century (Mark Twain, Edward Bellamy, the naturalistic novelists such as Norris) to understand America and its future in terms of alleged historical or cosmic forces, which had in fact very little historical content, which were far out of touch with whatever of historical actuality these writers perceived. Whitman's most concerted attempt to understand America in its actuality was *Democratic Vistas*, of which the next chapter takes note.

In accounting for the poetic decline which so clearly belies Whitman's own idea that he was ranging along the high plateau of his life and capacity during the Washington days, one must not forget that after 1864 he was never entirely well. In the midsummer of that year, after a long stint of hospital work, he fell sick, and after writing to his mother about his "spells of deathly faintness and bad trouble in my head too, and sore throat," he journeyed to Brooklyn for a vacation. Although he soon recovered and returned to Washington, he suffered periodic illnesses until, after reading a novel of Bulwer-Lytton at night on February 22, 1873, at his desk in the Treasury Building, he returned to his room and, during the night, suffered his first paralytic shock. By late March Whitman had rallied enough so that he could resume a part of his work, but the plight of his mother, now enfeebled and living with his brother George at Camden, caused him continual anxiety. Alarmed at his mother's illness, Whitman arrived in Camden on May 20; she died May 23—his mother, "the most perfect and magnetic character, the rarest combination of practical, moral, and spiritual, and the least selfish, of all and any I have ever known, and by me O so much the most deeply loved." His mother's death, as Walt wrote to Pete Doyle, was "the great cloud of my life." Whitman settled down with his brother, living the life of a semi-invalid and occupying the room his mother had had.

CHAPTER V

"THE THEORY OF AMERICA"

LIKE ALL of Whitman's prophetic utterances, *Democratic Vistas* (1871) is a transcendental version of Jeffersonian-Jacksonian democracy, the credo which Whitman had more literally expressed in his earlier newspaper writings, particularly the editorials in the Brooklyn *Eagle* and *Times*. The idea of progress becomes the principle of the universe —as we look up from our provisional Pisgah we behold the orbic forms of a benevolent, self-purifying cosmos; as we lower our gaze the vistas out over the continent darken some-what and are populated with villages, rivers, fields of wheat, factories, mechanics, farmers, patient mothers, small property holders, town meetings—a notably if evanescently envisioned myth of social life.

The absence in *Democratic Vistas* of direct political recom-mendation may be traced to Whitman's lifelong distrust of government. It may also be traced to Whitman's disillusion with practical politics, which he had long since given up in disgust, saying, for example, that the presidents immediately preceding Lincoln had all been "deform'd, mediocre, snivel-ling, unreliable, false-hearted men." He had always believed that social reform was a matter of individual regeneration, was not a political but a moral and spiritual problem; and all the weakness and strength of this view are in *Democratic Vistas*. One may note, however, the passage where Whitman momentarily fears he has gone too far in rejecting politics and, even though "these savage, wolfish parties alarm me," urges young men to take up a political career.

The individualism Whitman always championed becomes in *Democratic Vistas* his doctrine of "personalism"; his life-long belief in free trade is spiritualized into a vision of international amity. The moral-prophetic office of the poet on which the *Vistas* insists, had, of course, already been insisted on in the 1855 Preface. But although in many ways *Democratic Vistas* is a restatement of old views, Whitman's strong reaction to the spectacle of the Grant Administration and the Gilded Age gives the piece a novel emphasis on the need for "more compaction and more moral identity" in what the author took to be perilously anarchic times, and it also accounts for the intense concern with "personalism" and the unprecedented urgency with which the great function of the "literatus" is asserted.

Democratic Vistas shares some of that indistinctness of outline which many people now seem to find in nineteenth-century social polemic, overladen as it often was by merely ethical and prophetic tendencies. Doubtless we miss a certain hardheaded but humane pragmatism in listening to the exhortations of Whitman, as we miss also a genuine sense of history. True, Whitman is capable of historical or political realism. He echoes Mill, Arnold, and Tocqueville in saying that no one ought to "debate to-day whether to hold on, attempting to lean back and monarchize, or to look forward and democratize—but *how*, and in what degree or part, most prudently to democratize." This is a simple observation, but it is also a breath of fresh air in an atmosphere that is sometimes oppressively thick. Whitman can even write that "we do not (at least I do not) put it either on the ground that the People, the masses, even the best of them, are, in their latent or exhibited qualities, essentially sensible and good—nor on the ground of their rights; but that good or bad, rights or no rights, the democratic formula is the only safe and preservative one for coming times," and this is gratifyingly free of jargon.

Whitman can say, too, "I hail with joy the oceanic, variegated, intense practical energy, the demand for facts, even the business materialism of the current age, our States. But woe to the age or land in which these things, movements, stopping at themselves, do not tend to ideas." Matthew Arnold himself might almost have written this. And the *Vistas* is in fact much closer to the general run of nineteenth-century Anglo-Saxon social prophecy than it is to the French enlightenment, Hegel, or Marx. It is true that Whitman fancied himself as something of a Hegelian and even wrote to Edward Dowden that in *Democratic Vistas*, he meant to "project . . . an entirely new breed of authors, poets, American, comprehensive, Hegelian, Democratic, religious." But Whitman's second-hand idea of Hegel is indistinguishable from the loose transcendentalist dialectic he had found in Emerson, and perhaps Carlyle, and had "promulged" in "Song of Myself."

The truth is that *Democratic Vistas* is a kind of American version of Arnold's *Culture and Anarchy*, despite the fact that Whitman and Arnold were very little disposed to believe they had anything in common and despite Whitman's attacks, in the *Vistas*, on "culture" and "the grand style," both of which he understood to be mere dilettantism. But do not both authors believe that the present danger in their countries is anarchy, that modern man places too great a faith in the mere machinery of legislation, that lively, elevating ideas should be current, that the middle class is the one to rely on, that aggressive assertions of material progress, including the mass production of vulgar literature may cloak a virulent moral sickness, that poetry has a very broad function, including that of religion? In one important respect Whitman was more "Arnoldian" than Arnold—to the extent, that is, that his sense of things remained rather too exclusively ethical and literary and lacked historical objectivity.

But *Democratic Vistas* is broadly American in spirit, not only in its native idealism, its large hopefulness, its lack of concern with the limitations of life, its disinclination to understand that society is based on contradictions which may be humanly tragic but that nevertheless "freedom," "personalism," "compaction and moral identity" cannot be understood or exist outside of society. Also characteristic of our native mind is the swinging back and forth from minute realism to the most ultimate and ideal of considerations. Whitman finds it perfectly natural on one page to imply that democracy may turn out to be unworkable but that history has stuck us with it and we must face the fact and, on another page, to say that democracy should not be confined to the political sphere but should be extended, like a redemptive spirit, to every part of life including manners, religion, and literature, as well as the Army and Navy. Again, Whitman can be exact and particular in his denunciation of the social scene but the closest he gets to describing what an admirable American society might be is his pleasing but impalpable vision of "some pleasant western settlement or town, where a couple of hundred best men and women, of ordinary worldly status, have by luck been drawn together."

The fundamental contradiction of *Democratic Vistas* is, of course, one of which Whitman is intensely aware: "This idea of perfect individualism it is indeed that deepest tinges and gives character to the idea of the aggregate. For it is mainly or altogether to serve independent separation that we favor a strong generalization, consolidation." Just how the claims of the individual and those of the aggregate are to be harmoniously reconciled without destroying either is certainly a basic political question. More strongly than anywhere else in his writings, Whitman urges the importance of national unity. But like most Americans of his time Whitman, although capable of understanding unity as consisting in a commonalty of tradition and experience, could not understand that this felt unity must express itself in laws and institutions evolving in history, that it must be made practicable by the social intelligence. Doubtless the Grant Administration exhibited few enough of these unifying political forces. But Whitman's mind was incapable of supplying them. Instead he offered his old solution: the ideal of "perfect comradeship."

It would surely have outraged Whitman to have been told that *Democratic Vistas* shows less knowledge of political realities and a weaker sense of history than *Culture and Anarchy* (to take up again the comparison), or that in so far as he is political at all he is, in an important sense, more conservative than Arnold. Yet both these propositions are true. As for the relative conservatism of these two writers, we have only to ask what, in the *Vistas* and in *Culture and Anarchy*, is taken to be the central and determining fact about the societies to which they refer. The given fact in Arnold's book is historical change of the most portentous sort, for Arnold is as impressed as Tocqueville by the historic forward march of the democratization of the Western world. This change entails a radical departure from all past experience. Arnold's conservatism is confined to his attempt to modify the course of democratization in accordance with the traditional values he cherishes. But he is clearly committed to basic changes.

The given fact in *Democratic Vistas* is a set of American beliefs and attitudes—"the American programme"—which was "put on record" once and for all in "the compacts of the Declaration of Independence" and "the Federal Constitution." The business of poets is not to "criticize life" but to reveal the given "compacts," to furnish the "archetypes" of thought and experience implied by what providence has decreed America to be. From this point of view, Whitman will not even admit that historical change is possible. For despite all his appeals to the future greatness of America there is nothing in this future which is not merely a further revelation of the totally adequate dispensation vouchsafed to Americans at the birth of the Republic. Change is understood as a progressive discovery of something already given, though not at first correctly or clearly perceived in its entirety. If Arnold tends to think of England as hastening perilously into the problematical future, Whitman thinks of America as exploring her "exhaustless mines of the richest ore" and as furnishing out the future with that which has already been given—a future which cannot help being better than the present because it will be a fuller, a more valid realization of what providence decreed America to be in 1776, Whitman seems to think, when to all intents and purposes history stopped, its final purpose of outdating "feudalism" and announcing democracy having been accomplished. History is, as it were, a kind of great mother whose divine duty it was to bear a democratic son to succeed a tyrannical father. Thus the true prophet (says Whitman in *Specimen Days*) does not so much "predict" as "reveal and outpour" the "inner, divine spontaneities" of the soul. One of the paradoxes of Whitman's work is that prophecy as a wild, spontaneous poetic outflowing is the source both of the radical, utopian indeterminacy of "Song of Myself" and the fundamentally conservative political ideas of *Democratic Vistas*. And this paradox is, of course, not only Whitman's. Probably more often than not it is the function of prophecy itself to be emotionally and poetically wild, rhapsodic, and visionary while maintaining conservative political or religious views. At any rate, this paradox is native to the democratic mind. Most Americans, certainly most of our great writers past and present, can see themselves in one form or another in that "conservative Christian anarchist" Henry Adams declared himself to be.

Democratic Vistas is not the great piece of radical social ideology it has sometimes been called. Like most American social thinking, it is conservative, individualistic, and unhistorical. But if this native habit of mind, together with the author's too exclusive preoccupation with moral, spiritual, and literary values, weakened his grasp of political reality, his appraisal of the individual is acute and persuasive, and his account of literature as the force which must reconcile individual and aggregate, though absurd to the extent that it is taken as a direct political recommendation, has its relevance to social actualities.

That celebration of the "simple separate person" which Whitman had come to call "personalism" is the glory of *Democratic Vistas*. "Personalism" is merely Whitman's new word for "identity," but in *Democratic Vistas* the idea is insisted on with a new urgency and beheld with a new clarity. Whitman's greatness had always rested in his ability to describe the plight and career of the self in all of its "singleness and normal simplicity and separation," as he says in the *Vistas*, as well as in the astonishing and ever novel modes of its entanglement with the world in which it exists. In "Song of Myself" we have the comic dance of the self becoming alternately entangled in and extricated from the complicated web of human life and the universe. Here the self was conceived as a kind of coy, elusive, democratic Pan. In "Out of the Cradle" and "As I Ebb'd with the Ocean of Life" the poet had chanted his great dirges on the separation of the self, the plight and pathos of singleness. Here the self had been conceived psychologically and metaphysically. In *Democratic Vistas* the self is intuitively perceived as an irreducible fact of personal and social experience, not immediately as a *political* fact, but as a fact without which there can be no humane politics:

There is, in sanest hours, a consciousness, a thought
that rises independent, lifted out from all else, calm, like
the stars, shining eternal. This is the thought of identity—yours for you, whoever you are, as mine for me.
Miracle of miracles, beyond statement, most spiritual
and vaguest of earth's dreams, yet hardest basic fact,
and only entrance to all facts. In such devout hours, in
the midst of the significant wonders of heaven and earth
(significant only because of the Me in the center),
creeds, conventions, fall away and become of no account before this simple idea. Under the luminousness
of real vision, it alone takes possession, takes value. Like
the shadowy dwarf in the fable, once liberated and
look'd upon, it expands over the whole earth, and
spreads to the roof of heaven.

It is hardly possible to imagine a more vital and necessary intuition than this. For surely one may judge whether or not a
nation can be called civilized by the extent to which it is able
to keep this "most spiritual and vaguest of earth's dreams,
yet hardest basic fact" vitally operative. The conditions of the
modern world are not conducive to sustaining in the mind
"the quality of Being, in the object's self." Fewer and fewer
people either have or know how to value Whitman's sense of
how the sources of our being pour ever novel forms of vitality
into the self and of how the self can be sustained in a hostile
world.

Without at all discounting the incalculable value of Whitman's "personalism," one must nevertheless note that he
characteristically tries to make it do too much. Not having
anything like so clear an intuition of society or of history as
he has of the self, he believes only in the self and asks it to do
what society ought at least assist in doing. Thus "personalism" not only discovers and asserts the personal; it also, in

some unspecified realm of being, "fuses" men into "solidarity."

This is where literature comes in. The "literatuses" of the future will create the kind of instinctive national mind necessary to the resolution of the contradictions of democracy, the purification of its evils, the toughening of its moral and physical being, and the final establishment of the comradely ideal. Whitman believes that so far America has no "real literature" and has produced no literatuses. Apparently not even Emerson is a literatus, not to mention Cooper, Hawthorne, Poe, Thoreau, and Melville. What kind of literature is it that Whitman finds at once not existent and desirable?

The coming American literature must have native roots—art forms "touch a man closest (perhaps only actually touch him) . . . in their expression through autochthonic lights and shades." American poetry must be "bold, modern, and all-surrounding and kosmical"; it must illustrate the people and respond to the slang, the folkways, the vast spectacle of the expanding country; it should not respond to the "covert, the lurid, the maleficent, the devil, the grim estimates inherited from the Puritans, hell, natural depravity, and the like"; it must be morally sound (not, of course, prudish) and appeal to the "absolute Conscience"; it must treat of nature in her universal, cosmical aspect and as the manifestation of the All; it must culminate in "metaphysics"—that is, in an inquiry into "the mysteries of the spiritual world, the soul itself, and the question of the immortal continuation of our identity"; finally it should possess "great poems of death."

In these prescriptions for American literature Whitman is very far from reality. Although his literary ideal corresponds to his own worst poems, it corresponds only partly to his best. Although it is a fair description of much of our second-rate literature, it has little relation to the first-rate either before

Whitman or after. If American writing at its best was to be seen in such works as *Huckleberry Finn, The Red Badge of Courage, The Sound and the Fury, The Sun Also Rises*, or the poems of Frost, Eliot, and Stevens, the recommendations of *Democratic Vistas* are clearly out of touch with the American literary spirit. It is only such a work as Frank Norris' *The Octopus* that fulfills Whitman's specifications, and it is a pretty piece of irony that in that novel Presley, the would-be bard who speaks for Norris and wants to celebrate the expanding West in a rhapsodic poem, has apparently never heard of Whitman and delights in the idea that he may be known as the greatest American poet since Bryant.

One must notice that although Whitman speaks of "real literature" and wants a literary response to the realities of American life, he is certainly not demanding what since Stephen Crane and Howells we have been calling "realism" and "naturalism." And although there is a vigorous reforming note in his prophecy and although a connection is made between the People and literature, he is very far from urging "social realism," let alone "socialist realism" or "proletarian literature." At one point he actually urges writers to confront and oppose "the growing excess and arrogance of realism"; to be sure, he is not speaking technically of "literary realism," but the remark is encompassing enough to be relevant. And elsewhere he urges "no useless attempt to repeat the material creation, by daguerreotyping the exact likeness." It is thus only by example and in the limited ways we have noted above, in speaking of *Drum Taps*, that Whitman is a genuine precursor of modern realism.

Whitman of course asks too much of literature, as he does of "personalism," when he seems to hope that it can resolve the contradictions of democracy by furnishing archetypal images of perfect democratic persons and exploring the modes of human community. The literatus of democratic times, he says, has an even higher calling than the epic poet and prophet of "feudal" times. His task is harder because not only must he create the mythic archetypes of democracy—to take the place of Adam and Eve, Moses, Achilles, Prometheus, Arthur, Milton's Satan, Don Quixote, Shakespeare's Hamlet, Richard II, and Lear; he must also furnish all the spiritual guidance formerly provided by priests. We do know, to be sure, that Shelley's idea about poets being the unacknowledged legislators of the world is not mere illusion. Literature, even when it is abstruse and difficult, as Whitman's poetry often is, has its ways of entering into the national mind, a national mind like our own—at once so unformed and so Alexandrian—not excepted. And we know that the shape and emphasis of political institutions are determined by shared, unconscious patterns of thought. The great writer has his effect on these, even if he is so little read as Walt Whitman. But the fact remains that the "literatus" who creates democratic archetypes as Whitman speaks of them has turned out to be someone like Stephen Vincent Benét—whose archetypes are synthetic products unhappily similar to the other products of our merchandising culture.

The most that can be said in defense of Whitman's program for literature is that literature does in truth deal with and exhibit modes of human community other than the mere idea of equality, which had always been the theoretical basis of Whitman's "adhesive" love of comrades. In *Democratic Vistas*, he had come to fear that equality was producing vulgarity and timidity, and that "a sort of dry and flat Sahara" was appearing in the midst of what ideally should be a various and energetic society. It is to Whitman's credit first, that he saw this to be true and, second, that he was not content merely to urge, as a cure, a more exalted equality. He does not, of course, abandon his faith in equality. He turns elsewhere in an attempt to understand how human experience may be shared and community formed without reducing life to a faceless uniformity. If we wish he had posited a vigorous, various, but harmonious political order, we must nevertheless observe that he was not entirely amiss in looking to literature, part of whose special prowess it is to seek out the difficult grounds of human commonalty.

Democratic Vistas impresses the reader with its many defects before it convinces him that it overcomes them. The piece is ill organized and sometimes otiose. The language burgeons outrageously. One can decipher and accept a reference to nature's "kosmical, antiseptic power" or to history as a series of "idiocratic transfers." But there isn't much excuse for saying of "the third stage" of American history (the first is the laying of the political foundations, the second the consolidation of material progress) that "rising out of the previous ones, to make them and all illustrious, I, now, for one, promulge, announcing a native expression-spirit, getting into form, adult, and through mentality, for these States, self-contain'd, different from others, more expansive," and so on. There is less positively brilliant writing in *Democratic Vistas* than there is in the Preface of 1855, less that is in its way immediately authentic and final. At the same time the *Vistas* makes a more extensive use of the specific virtues of prose than does the Preface, and it has consequently a sustained polemical eloquence and the amplitude of effect and incident which are proper to a meditative and summary as well as a prophetic piece in which the author is reflecting on problems that have occupied a lifetime. There is great eloquence in the passages deploring America's "hollowness of heart"; a sharp satirical pleasure in the author's attacks on "flippancy, tepid amours, weak infidelism, small aims"; the old ability to catalogue the multifarious aspects of the city in such a way that the catalogue becomes a vision. And there is spiritedness and clairvoyance in what is doubtless the most valuable function of *Democratic Vistas*—its assertion of "the fresh, eternal qualities of Being."

There is much surface disorder in the loose and impassioned argument of Whitman's essay. Yet this seems a minor fault. Indeed, from a modern point of view, one may feel that a graver fault is the lack of an adequate sense of disorder. Like much amateur philosophy and much nineteenth-century social polemic *Democratic Vistas* strikes the modern reader as being too simply and schematically reasoned, as having underneath its surface sense of wildness, indeterminacy, and doubt a too simple, even a complacent, faith in the rational unities of democratic society, which in practice meant a too simple faith in the status quo. History, in so far as it is present at all, is regarded as maternal and beneficent. It therefore has no hazards and can be counted on to foster democracy. "The distinguishing event of my time," as Whitman called the Civil War, conspired to turn his mind too exclusively to modes of reconciliation, comradeship, and unity, and partly as a consequence of the one supreme tragic crisis of our civilization, he failed, like most of his contemporaries, to conceive of radically disastrous historical crises and dilemmas. He knew that the life of the self, of the individual, might involve such crises. But he did not believe that the same might be true of the history of nations, at least not of America and the nations of the future.

Still *Democratic Vistas* is an admirable and characteristic diatribe. And if one is sorry that in it Whitman is unable to conceive the extreme crises of society, one is certain that no society would be tolerable whose citizens could not find refreshment in its buoyant democratic idealism.

CHAPTER VI

"NOTES OF A HALF-PARALYTIC"

WHITMAN THOUGHT that *Specimen Days*, which he published in 1882, might well be the "most wayward, spontaneous, fragmentary book ever written." The book is certainly wayward and fragmentary, and although it is not always spontaneous, it is often engaging and has been somewhat neglected by students of Whitman. The implied intention of *Specimen Days*, like that of *Leaves of Grass*, is autobiographical. But like *Leaves of Grass*, it is autobiographical only spasmodically and "indirectly." The book falls into three parts: a short introductory section devoted to reminiscence of the Whitman family, the poet's ancestors, the homestead, Long Island scenes, and early experiences; a longer middle section of notes and vignettes from the war years; and a still longer concluding section of notes on nature, ideas, and representative men the poet has known or admired.

The personal reminiscences at the beginning of the book are tantalizing in their extreme sketchiness and the air of mystery, of closely guarded secrets, which the writer casts over them. But there is a certain elegiac dignity in the meditations of the poet as he sits "on an old grave . . . on the burial hill of the Whitmans of many generations," fleeting as these meditations are. And there are some memorable passages of genre painting (of the kind Matthiessen discusses at length in

American Renaissance), such as: "Inside the outer bars or beach this south bay is everywhere comparatively shallow; of cold winters all thick ice on the surface. As a boy I often went forth with a chum or two, on those frozen fields, with hand sled, ax, and eel-spear, after messes of eels."

Whitman's notes on the Civil War are, of course, precious items in the national archives. Their literary quality is unquestionable; they always strike the reader as being so immediately authentic that commentary would be superfluous. Compared with Whitman's other prose, they are terse, graphic, and understated. We are told by the writer that most of these notes "are verbatim copies of those lurid and blood-smutch'd little note-books" which he kept with him on the battlefield and in the hospitals. We are given strongly realistic pictures of the suffering of the soldiers, the bad conditions that prevailed in the hospitals, the corruption these conditions induced. But we are told also that the writer has seen such things as cannot be written down and that "the real war will never get in the books." Not much interested in taking sides, the writer studies violence and suffering in themselves. So that his style and his attitude toward what he is writing entitle Whitman to be called the first of the legendary war reporters, the literary ancestor of Ambrose Bierce, Stephen Crane, and Ernest Hemingway. Many of the realistic passages in *The Red Badge of Courage* are anticipated in *Specimen Days*, and this is even truer of J. W. DeForest's fine novel *Miss Ravenel's Conversion* (1867). It should be clear, however, that although the War seemed to Whitman "the distinguishing event of my time," he did not, either in his war notes or elsewhere, come to understand life in terms of violence, as did Bierce, Crane, and Hemingway. For various personal and historical reasons, his fascination with war and death was not, like theirs, overt, flamboyant, and active; it remained passive, mystical, and sacrificial. But like the later war correspondents he prided himself on being able to say, "I am the man, I suffer'd, I was there."

Although the war sketches do not violate the general intention of *Specimen Days,* they are different in tone from the random nature jottings and reflective passages which constitute the bulk of the volume. In this (the third) part of the book Whitman's intention, suitable to a "half-Paralytic" but necessary to life itself, is to relax the will and renew contact with plain, natural things. "To unstring the divine bow, so tense, so long," he cries; ". . . to bring people back from their persistent strayings and sickly abstractions, to the costless average, divine, original concrete." "The trick is," as he says, "to tone your wants and tastes low down enough, and make much of negatives, and of mere daylight and the skies." "Literature flies so high" that one must "restore" one's "book" to the "equilibrium of concrete outdoor Nature." Whitman imparts a gently stoic mood to *Specimen Days,* and the appropriate emblem of this book is not the teeming, many-tongued grass but the rugged cedar-plum that grows in "sand and bleak side spots" and is distinguished by "its silence, its equable acceptance of winter's cold, of summer's heat, of rain or drouth." In a mood to write about "little things" he had "either never seen . . . to such advantage or had never noticed," Whitman produced a small body of charming nature notes such as the following:

> *June 19th,* 4 to 6½, P.M.—Sitting alone by the creek—solitude here, but the scene bright and vivid enough—the sun shining, and quite a fresh wind blowing (some heavy showers last night), the grass and trees looking their best—the clare-obscure of different greens, shadows, half-shadows, and the dappling glimpses of the water, through recesses—the wild flageolet-note of a quail near by—the just-heard fretting of some hylas down there in the pond—crows

cawing in the distance—a drove of young hogs rooting in soft ground near the oak under which I sit—some come sniffing near me, and then scamper away, with grunts. And still the clear notes of the quail—the quiver of leaf-shadows over the paper as I write—the sky aloft, with white clouds, and the sun well declining to the west—the swift darting of many sand-swallows coming and going, their holes in a neighboring marl-bank—the odor of the cedar and oak, so palpable, as evening approaches—perfume, color, the bronze-and-gold of nearly ripen'd wheat—clover-fields, with honey-scent—the well-up maize, with long and rustling leaves—the great patches of thriving potatoes, dusky green, fleck'd all over with white blossoms—the old, warty, venerable oak above me—and ever, mix'd with the dual notes of the quail, the soughing of the wind through some near-by pines.

As I rise for return, I linger long to a delicious song-epilogue (is it the hermit-thrush?) from some bushy recess off there in the swamp, repeated leisurely and pensively over and over again. This, to the circle-gambols of the swallows flying by dozens in concentric rings in the last rays of sunset, like flashes of some airy wheel.

At one point Whitman says of such jottings as these that they were intended as "hints and data of a Nature-poem that should carry one's experiences a few hours, commencing at noon-flush, and so through the after part of the day—I suppose led to such idea by my own life-afternoon now arrived." Which may serve to raise the question of whether or to what extent Whitman actually is a nature poet or a nature writer of any sort.

The *Whitman Handbook* instructs us that our poet is "a great nature lover" and that "nature plays a prominent part in all his poems." And there is no doubt that Whitman thought of himself as a nature writer just as surely as he thought that all poetry should be autobiographical. But these were among the most conventional of all nineteenth-century ideas about literature and Whitman was often subject to conventional ideas. The fact is that, as I have suggested before, Whitman's capacity for direct and close observation of nature is only intermittently in operation. His catalogues of natural objects often sound as if he had culled them (as he often *did* cull them) from books and newspapers rather than from nature; his nature scenes often give the impression of being observed at an exhibition of paintings rather than in the countryside. The intermittent operation of Whitman's faculty for direct natural observation makes us doubt whether he was much of a nature poet. But it did give him one advantage— namely, that he was always *discovering* nature as if for the first time, and this enhanced that sense of novelty, the sense that there *are* new things under the sun, which is one of Whitman's strong points. One of the charms of *Specimen Days* is the mild pleasure of beholding with Whitman things which he "had never noticed before" in his sixty-two years.

There are many complicated cultural and intellectual influences tending to persuade the American literary mind away from the steady contemplation of nature (so that, as it would seem, we have had to establish a separate group of "nature writers" from Thoreau and Burroughs to Joseph Wood Krutch to deal with the situation). This is certainly not the place to test at length Tocqueville's assertion that "democratic nations may amuse themselves for a while with considering the productions of Nature; but they are only excited in reality by a survey of themselves." Yet *Specimen Days* is a test case. And despite its many passages of authentic naturalism and despite the expressed intention of the author to seek out "the costless, average, divine original concrete," the general motion of his mind is toward transcendental and symbolic formulations.

It might be well to remark again that Whitman is peculiarly urban in his mentality and that he looks at nature as a city man does. He speaks the plain truth near the end of *Specimen Days* when he says, "I find the human and objective atmosphere of New York City and Brooklyn more affiliative to me than any other." And the carefully framed word-picture of himself as he sun-bathes by a stream in the countryside near Camden—"Nude with Straw Hat and Portable Chair" —is more akin to the sensibility of a Parisian painter than to that of a nature poet.

When Whitman is not seeing in nature ready-made pictures, he is likely to be looking through nature to the soul within—"the all-basis, the nerve, the great-sympathetic, the plenum within humanity, giving stamp to everything" and remaining "necessarily invisible." This reminds one of the Emerson who says, "From the earth as a shore, I look out into that silent sea. I seem to partake its rapid transformations: the active enchantment reaches my dust, . . ." And it reminds one of Frost's "Neither Out Far Nor in Deep," wherein

> The people along the sand
> All turn and look one way.
> They turn their back on the land.
> They look at the sea all day.

Or of Melville's Ishmael, who observes "thousands and thousands of mortal men . . . posted like silent sentinels" around Manhattan and "fixed in ocean reveries." Or of the sea, "the float forever held in solution," in Whitman's own poems. Or of the "great well" in the Gulf over which the fishermen pass in Hemingway's *The Old Man and the Sea.* Many other kinds of image have been used to convey this transcendental view of nature, but these sea images should serve to illustrate how very strong in American writers is the tendency to find among the objects of nature only an occasion for responding to the hypnotic spell of the unconscious and the infinite. Not that one can disapprove of a turn of mind which has produced so much fine literature; I merely wish to point out how little this turn of mind is consonant with "nature poetry."

Instructive as it is, one cannot quite agree with F. O. Matthiessen's account of Whitman in *American Renaissance* in so far as this depends on his general assertion that Whitman improves as a writer to the extent that he is able to observe closely the particularities of nature and "to translate man into nature." Determined to find in Whitman a precursor of modern materialistic naturalism, Matthiessen came to feel that the importance of Whitman's writing is that it shows his mind to have moved "from transcendentalism back to a kind of materialism." It is true, as we have noticed above, that Whitman is often at his best when he is observing particulars, not only in *Specimen Days* but elsewhere—"And limitless are leaves stiff or drooping in the fields, / And brown ants in the little wells beneath them." Yet we have also noticed that his observations of things are likely to be second hand or, as Thoreau complained, mere "brick," unless they are transfigured by a vision which makes them items in eternity or forms fresh from the unconscious. So that we can hardly understand Whitman's peculiar genius as the ability "to translate man into nature." This will apply only to his elegiac mood, his sense of annihilation and death. It would be truer to say that as a general thing he translates nature into man, that he makes nature dance to the tune of the human spirit—that for him, as Quentin Anderson says of Emerson, "nature was a set of correspondences exemplifying our nature, not its own." Whitman's view of nature is profoundly equivocal or, to put it more positively, it is interesting, contradictory, and vital.

So it is in *Specimen Days*. But this work is distinguished from the author's other writings by the fact that the close notations are the only really interesting parts of those pages which deal with nature. Where he essays to treat nature more imaginatively, he quickly falls back on purely conventional and "literary" figures. Roosters are "chanticleers," a bird is a "feather'd recluse," the hills are "swathed with verdure," the dawn is "venus-heralded," butterflies are "beautiful, spiritual insects! straw-color'd Psyches!"—and here one recalls the photograph Whitman liked so much, taken in his later years and showing him with a pensively extended forefinger whereon is tied with a barely perceptible thread a cardboard butterfly.

Of the random "thoughts and jottings" on literary and philosophical matters in *Specimen Days* those on Carlyle are much the most vivid (Whitman is merely tiresome in his conventionalized pronouncements of Emerson, Longfellow, Bryant, and Whittier—"the mighty four who stamp this first American century with its birthmarks of poetic literature"— one had not imagined that Longfellow was a "literatus." Of more interest, however, is the nicely limned piece on Poe, who is a significant specimen of the "disease called humanity"). The same mixture of attraction and repulsion that Whitman had always manifested in his thoughts about Carlyle are manifest here, intensified by Carlyle's death in 1881. "We surely learn deepest from unlikeness," says Whitman, affirming that although Carlyle's books are "feudal at the core," they "afford ever-valuable lessons and affinities to democratic America." Whitman writes that he is forced finally to reject the teachings of Carlyle because Carlyle did not recognize "the limits" of his view of modern times, a view immensely valuable as a critique of democracy but dangerous, because feudal, pessimistic and "world-decadent," as a positive program. Intellectually, Hegel must be preferred to Carlyle, since his positive philosophical prescriptions seem to tally with the spirit of democracy and the "Metaphysics" of the New World. This being so, how to account for the "inexplicable *rapport*" between "our United States" and Carlyle, "the most erudite and sincere mind of Europe"? And Whitman admits, "I am certainly at a loss to account for it all as affecting myself."

The strong identification with Carlyle one feels Whitman to be making was of a deeper sort than that he had long recognized. He had always seen that they were both "metaphysical," that they shared the Hebraic spirit of prophecy, that they both wrote in a "strange wild way." But now he finds an opportunity in writing about Carlyle to register, with the tag-end of his energies, one last impassioned protest against the stultifying *Leaves-of-Grass* and Good-Gray-Poet cult the disciples had built up around him. And I would suggest that it is this impulse one hears in his expostulations about how much one can learn from "unlikeness" and in his interpolated outcry that "Michel Angelo invoked heaven's special protection against his friends and affectionate flatterers; palpable foes he could manage for himself." Only a few months later Whitman was to write to Richard Bucke, who was about to publish an official biography (to the composition of which Whitman himself appears to have made substantial contributions), that "the character you give me is not the true one in the main—I am by no means the benevolent, equable, good happy creature you portray." But even though no truer words were ever spoken, Whitman was ready to "let that pass." Yet one part of him bridled, was not inclined to let it pass, and found indirect expression in the remarks on Carlyle. These praise Carlyle for being the sort of vital, contradictory man Whitman himself had once been. Carlyle is "a representative author" in whom one sees the "significant hints of our stormy era, its fierce paradoxes, its din, and its struggling parturition periods." One sees "two conflicting agonistic elements" in Carlyle, "sometimes pulling him different ways like wild horses. He was a cautious, conservative Scotchman, fully aware what a foetid gas-bag much of modern radicalism is; but then his great heart demanded reform, demanded change—often terribly at odds with his scornful brain." "It is time," Whitman writes, "the English-speaking people had some true idea about the verteber of genius, namely power"—and the implication surely is that the English-speaking people can learn this either from Carlyle or from Whitman. True, Carlyle lacks the democratic "soul-sight and root-center." But there is something great in his perception of "this multifarious, mad chaos of fraud, frivolity, hoggishness—this revel of fools, and incredible make-believe and general unsettledness, we call *the world*." Whitman thinks that there may be a kind of indirect virtue in the fact that one's mind is haunted by "the spectre of world-destruction"; and he adds, "Greek scholars, I believe, find the same mocking and fantastic apparition attending Aristophanes, his comedies." And in this way what might be called the "agonistic Whitman" voices a late, enfeebled denial of the Good Gray Poet. It is only a little difficult to hear him heatedly mumbling his protest in the thick atmosphere of the bland, emasculate, pseudo-messianic ideal imposed upon him by his admirers and on the whole acquiesced in by himself.

That Whitman did indeed grow vague, maundering, and bland during the twilight years of his life cannot be denied. Yet there was a kind of indestructible dignity as well as an aura of wistful comedy about the Whitman of the Camden years, despite the banalities, pretensions, and slowly accumulating evidences of mental and physical failure which one must also associate with these years. Even as he deteriorated under the assaults of disease, the "splendid old soul," as Mark Twain called him, was able as he had always been to confound those who deny both to his life and to his works the power of transforming the inchoate flow of experience into the ideal.

During the eleven years after 1873, Whitman lived as a boarder with his brother George, moving, after that, into a small house of his own on Mickle Street. Here he passed through several phases of increasing illness and momentary recovery. He continued to write poems, to revise and publish new editions of *Leaves of Grass*, and to publicize himself. He gave lectures and readings. He continued his practice of ferry and horsecar riding, except that now the city to which he journeyed was Philadelphia and that now he had to ease his partially paralyzed left leg along with a cane. He received pilgrims and admirers as he had been doing since the visit of Thoreau and Alcott in 1856, but now the visitors came in large numbers, many with the alarming gleam in the eye that betokens the Truth newly seen. He hobbled, too, into the countryside, staying sometimes in the summer with a farm family on Timber Creek and making the renewed connection with nature which he describes in *Specimen Days*.

One of the dubious activities of the last years was Whitman's conniving at or acquiescing in the solicitation of funds among English and American literary people—dubious because it is not clear that Whitman was by any means always on that brink of penury where the contributors supposed him to be. Some of the donors were surprised when Whitman died to learn that he had paid four thousand dollars for a tomb and that he had several thousand in the bank. A friend insisted that the vague old man had been mulcted by the monumentalist and that he was saving money for the maintenance of his brother Eddie, who still lived on in the asylum. Yet Mrs. Mary Davis, the devoted widow, who moved into

Whitman's house with all her furniture and kept house for him and endured the gossip of the neighbors and was understandably piqued because Whitman refused to marry her, was outraged when she received, according to the will, only five hundred dollars, and instituted a lawsuit. She had her point. At any rate, some of the disputed funds had come from very eminent donors, including Mark Twain, Andrew Carnegie, Tennyson, the Rossettis, Saintsbury, John Hay, St. Gaudens, Lowell, Norton, and Henry James.

Among Whitman's European visitors there were Sir Henry Irving, Edmund Gosse, Sir Edwin Arnold—and Oscar Wilde, whose demeanor seems to have been on this occasion grave and hushed. There was also a Russian anarchist—"clean, earnest, with a beautiful face, but too insistent," said Whitman. The young man had wanted Whitman to endorse his political views and had moved him to reflect that "I suppose I am radical his way, but I am not radical his way alone. Socialists, single tax men, communists, rebels of every sort and all sorts, come here . . . But I am not economically informed—I do not see the fine, even the coarse, points of difference between the contestants." Equally baffling was Mrs. Gilchrist, an English widow of pre-Raphaelite connections who had been an early reader of Whitman. After writing Whitman many impassioned letters which seemed to deal exclusively with matters of the spirit but implicitly suggested and then demanded matrimony, Mrs. Gilchrist arrived with her two children and settled in Philadelphia. Although this was undeniable proof of the power of Whitman's poetry to exert an effect on human affairs, it was not what the poet had had in mind. The situation called for tact and a kind of sanctified vagueness, and Whitman employed both to such good effect that Mrs. Gilchrist amicably returned, after a year or more, to England.

Being an inveterate self-lionizer, Whitman had few enough defenses against the increasingly lionizing civilization he

lived in during his last years. He was painted, sculpted, pho-
tographed, interviewed, and quoted as no one except perhaps Mark Twain and Shaw have been. He was flattered by
men like Dr. Bucke, who announced that his meeting with
Whitman had been the "turning point of my life" and who
wrote a biography of Whitman (possibly the "very greatest
man that the world had so far produced") and a book called
Cosmic Consciousness. It is perhaps no wonder that in his
last years Whitman's thinking grew more and more indistinguishable from the dull mysticism and naïve spiritual postur-
ings of those around him.

One of the most vigorous of the disciples was Horace Traubel, a young man of advanced socialist opinions who attached
himself to the aging poet. Traubel became Whitman's Bos-
well, and we have him to thank for the enormous and more or
less accurate stenographic report of conversations with Whitman in 1888 and 1889, four large volumes of which have so
far appeared under the general title *With Walt Whitman in
Camden.* The house to which Traubel made his daily visits
was a rather run-down, two-story, wooden affair. Whitman
received him, as he did all his guests, in his room on the second floor. Doubtless there was much in the appearance of the
poet to impress a disciple—the flowing white hair and beard,
the lace shirt collar, the scent of *eau de cologne* about the
massive, immobile body, the heavy-lidded gray-blue eyes, ab-
stracted, impersonal, appealing. And there was much to at-
tract a young bohemian in the disorderly room—the unmade
bed, the sheet-iron stove, the masses of papers and books
strewn about the floor, table and bed, the odd collection of
pictures and photos on the wall. As Whitman poked among
the papers with his cane in search of the manuscript copy of
a poem or a letter from an admirer (it might be the letter
Whitman was unable to read because it had been written
in French by Francis Viélé-Griffin to say that two of his

poems had been translated and published by Jules Laforgue), one's eye might come to rest on an opulent waistcoat
sent by Lady Mount Temple, the daughter of Palmerston, or
on the picture on the mantel showing Washington standing
among the clouds, welcoming Lincoln to heaven, and placing
a wreath on his head.

And if there was a certain irreclaimable miscellaneousness
about Whitman's room, the same may be said for the *pensées*
set down by Traubel. Yet the miscellaneousness, the variety
of topic touched upon, is mostly of the surface and one cannot
read very far in these volumes without being aware of a
rather deadly monotony which imposes itself wherever the
tone of Whitman's unique language and personality is not
felt. Whitman's injunction to Traubel was, "Be sure to write
about me honest: whatever you do do not prettify me; include
all the hells and damns." Traubel does not prettify the poet
and he cannot help conveying a good deal of the essential
quality of his subject. But this he does inadvertently, being
so literal-minded a disciple of Whitman that he is interested
in nothing except the great man's ideas. He is not much
abashed, apparently, when Whitman observes, "I don't know
but I might as well say for us all, as well as for myself, that
this is a sort of bankrupty court of ideas." He continues sol-
emnly to set down all the poet utters, no matter how embar-
rassing or banal it may be.

At its worst the literary discussion Traubel records is
merely a choosing up of sides according to who is or is not
"our man" or "a *Leaves-of-Grass* man"—Dr. Johnson is not a
Leaves-of-Grass man, nor is Shakespeare, Milton, or Dante.
Emerson is our man; he is elemental, democratic, despite his
New England austerity. Despite his feudalism, Tennyson is
our man (presumably because he once wrote a friendly letter
to Whitman); but one cannot tell about Mark Twain—he is
"not exactly against me: not for me either." (It is true, how-

ever, that Whitman himself usually treated this choosing up
of sides rather jocosely.)

Among the other *obiter dicta* on literary figures we have
those on Arnold (who belongs to "the great army of critics,
parlor apostles, worshippers of hangings, laces, and so forth
and so forth"), Henry James ("feathers to me"), Howells (of
whom Whitman rightly says that he was "unable to follow up
radically the lead of his rather remarkable intellect"), John
Stuart Mill ("I have never read Mill. . . . What did he
stand for, teach, saliently promulge?"), Thoreau (whose
"great fault was disdain"), Robert Ingersoll ("America don't
know how proud she should be of Ingersoll").

Among novelists Whitman was always partial to Scott and
Cooper as well as Dickens. "How much I am indebted to
Scott no one can tell," he remarks to Traubel, "but it has
permeated me through and through. If you could reduce the
Leaves to their elements you would see Scott unmistakably
active at the roots . . . I might say just about the same thing
about Cooper." He says that "I have read" the *Heart of Midlothian* "a dozen times or more" and that "I never forget
Natty Bumppo—he is from everlasting to everlasting." One
side of Whitman's temperament, which hardly appears in
Leaves of Grass, could always respond to the thickly populated romantic tapestries with their many examples of stoi-
cally virtuous womanhood which he found in Scott and
Cooper, "feudal" though these authors might be. But in what
sense Scott is active at the roots of the *Leaves* it is a little hard
to see, although we can make some sense of Whitman's idea
by recalling that his earliest poetic attempts were in the manner of Scott's ballads and that from the whole work of Scott
he might have got the idea of the "literatus"—that is, a cre-
ator of "autochthons" and archetypes which should both epit-
omize and guide the mind of a people. Perhaps Whitman felt
about Scott and Cooper as he did about Percy's *Reliques:* "It

takes you to the birth of man: it is always a young book."

One must certainly share Whitman's general feeling about American poets whose reputations in his own time were so much more lustrous than his: "I have felt they have not let go—have not been willing to let the demon work out its fate —have not believed enough in themselves." He found no free spirits among these "genteel little creatures" with their "perpetual, pistareen, paste-pot work" (as he had written in *Democratic Vistas*). Looking abroad for great modern spirits, Whitman hails Tolstoy and Victor Hugo because of the powerful way in which they communicate with the masses. More interestingly, he singles out Heine for praise: "Heine! Oh how great! . . . Heine was free—was one of the men who win by degrees. . . . The more you stop to look, to examine, the deeper seem the roots, the broader and higher the umbrage. . . . At times he plays with you with a deliberate, baffling sportiveness." Whitman tells Traubel that Arnold's essay on Heine is perhaps his only good one—good enough at least to have moved Whitman to exclamatory versions of Arnold's observations about "Heine's intense modernism, his absolute freedom, his utter rejection of stock classicism and stock romanticism, his bringing all things under the point of view of the nineteenth century" and about "his wonderful clearness, lightness, and freedom, united with such power of feeling, and width of range." Arnold's essay could hardly have failed to appeal to Whitman, with all its talk of "Initiators," of "the application of modern ideas to life," of the gaiety and wit which endured in Heine even in the long years of physical deterioration and pain after his paralytic stroke. As for the future, Whitman was confident that Heine had staying power, "was one of the men who win by degrees."

What Whitman responded to in Heine, or Arnold's idea of Heine, was a certain divine susceptibility to experience, an openness to the sources of spiritual energy, a free, doubting, disruptive approach to life, a certain accessibility to extreme modes of feeling from the most profound to the most "sportive." These are qualities in Whitman himself which one must value highly and which one must always be concerned to single out from his less admirable qualities—such as his famous receptivity or passiveness, which sometimes renders him not "divinely susceptible to experience" but merely at the mercy of its undifferentiated flux and such as the solipsistic nature of his larger assertions about the world, betokening as these sometimes do an unstable grasp of certain ranges of reality and history of which a more profoundly organized mind would not be guilty. Whitman's divine susceptibility to experience was a priceless gift to our culture, a culture, as Lawrence says, in which a "tight mental allegiance [is] given to a morality which the passional self repudiates." Whitman was the "first to break the mental allegiance," says Lawrence. Allegiances we must have, but, as Whitman knew, they must be endlessly reconstituted out of the passional life.

Whitman's pronouncements on politics are rather baffling, but only on the surface. A vigorous socialist, Traubel liked to needle Whitman a good deal about politics. He complained that the great man was too conservative and that he was too ready to dismiss radicals as "doctrinaires and partisans." And even though Whitman might feel a kinship with a Russian anarchist and declare himself a radical, he was just as likely under other circumstances to call himself a conservative. He calls himself a "radical" very much in the same spirit as that in which all Americans now regard themselves as "liberals," or did until it recently became respectable among intellectuals to speak of oneself as "conservative." There is nothing in the Traubel conversations to indicate any change in Whitman from the libertarian conservatism of *Democratic Vistas*. The real Whitman speaks when he says to Traubel: "I am not afraid of conservatism, not afraid of going too slow, of being held back: rather I often wonder if we are not going ahead too swiftly—whether it's not good to have the radicalities, progresses, reforms, restrained . . . we must hold our horses . . . we must not rush aimlessly ahead." There was in fact no change in Whitman's basic political ideas after his first practical experience as an editorialist and minor Democratic politician in the 1840's had added to the Jeffersonian tradition of the family an abiding skepticism about reform and reformers. And even though he became a Free-Soiler and later voted for Lincoln, he always spoke scornfully of abolitionists like Garrison and Phillips. His understanding of the depth of human suffering and the difficulty of reform was enhanced by his observations of the degradation of the poorer classes, both Negro and white, during his sojourn in New Orleans. Whitman was staunchly of the middle class ("the most valuable class in any community," he wrote in the Brooklyn *Times*), and no less so in his illusions than in his practical sagacity and instinctive conservatism. There will always be a sense in which the Open Road is only an extension of Myrtle Street in Brooklyn, where the Whitmans and other small property-owning families lived during a part of Whitman's youth.

One of the historic illusions of the middle class has been what later skeptics have come to call the "myth of the proletariate." And not all of Whitman's political canniness could save him from this. Moncure Conway was the first to observe in Whitman (after visiting him in 1857) a "Quaker" illusion about his kinship with the masses and about the self-reforming powers of the people. And some of Whitman's comments to Traubel on literature and the masses, like many nineteenth-century utterances, have the look, by hindsight, of what was to be known as Stalinism, that master illusion of the middle class. There is something of this in Whitman's adulation of Carlyle because although not a progressive he accurately expresses "world-decadence." There is something of it in his idea of Hegel, Victor Hugo, and Tolstoy, the latter of whom he calls "a world force, an immense vehement first energy driving to the fulfillment of a great purpose." And then there is his idea that literature is "a means to an end. . . . Literature is big only in one way—when used as an aid in the growth of the humanities—a furthering of the cause of the masses— a means whereby men may be revealed to each other as brothers." Pronouncements of this sort represent the side of Whitman known to or imagined by political militancy on the "left," from the portentous progressivism of Parrington to the propaganda of world communism. But this is merely to say that in some limited ways Whitman's political thinking suffered from the corruption which has tainted and to a great extent destroyed all modern political thought. On the whole Whitman remains an old-fashioned libertarian, and the attempt to claim him for the world revolution will always be spurious.

If Traubel's volumes are only intermittently interesting as source books of ideas, they are almost always moving when we catch a glimpse of Whitman himself or when, in answer to some question, he talks about himself. There is his remark to Baker, the male nurse whom he required after May of 1888 and who had suggested that he take a bath: "I am too weak; I am fragile enough to break." And then, spying a huge tin tub that had been brought in, he cries "Christ a'mighty! What's that?" Or he would say "I'm turned clear off—off my keel—am badly shaken. I seem to see things all right with my mind but my body won't see things at all." And, gazing at a copy of *Leaves of Grass*, to which he was still adding annexes: "There's the book—the dear book—forever waiting— and I seem to be more feeble than ever." And, "I notice that everybody looks at me asquint, as if something was about to happen . . . but I'm not at all agreed to it just yet." He lived until Saturday afternoon, March 26, 1891, when he died of pneumonia and complications, after many months of pain.

I have no concluding moral to propose. I do not intend to brandish Whitman at the New Critics or at any other critics, or to suggest that he is an unsuspected precursor of the New Conservatism (if there is such a thing) or of any other school or movement. As I understand the drift of contemporary opinion, something more fundamental is at stake—whether as a literary and cultural force Whitman is dead or alive. Students, young readers, whether or not they are acquainted with the opinions of our most advanced critics seem generally to agree with these critics in requiring of Whitman, as they never would of Blake, or Yeats, or Donne, that he should prove his case as a poet. Nor do these young people or these critics think highly of Whitman as a polemicist, prophet, or annotator of specimen days—had Whitman, after all, the sense of evil?

These attitudes are beginning to change, however, and new ways of understanding Whitman, or the rediscovery of old ways, are clearly beginning to reinstate him. We need not be thrown off the track any longer because of the notorious fact that wherever Whitman's influence has been most direct it has been most deplorable—as on the Sandburgs, the Benéts, the Thomas Wolfes, even the Hart Cranes. This is of little interest as against the fact that in spirit and in language Whitman has become a part of our literary heritage almost without our knowing it and perhaps against our will, so that no literate reader can now read T. S. Eliot (to take a poet very unlike Whitman) without, betimes, feeling the presence of Whitman—in this or that reference to the lilac, the poignant song of the thrush, the items of city life, annihilation or re-birth in the sea which, as Eliot says, "is all about us." Nor can such a reader be anything but fascinated by Wallace Stevens' investigation of Whitman's sensibility in his "Like Decorations in a Nigger Cemetery." Nor can such a reader forget that his sense of Whitman's vitality in the literary tradition has been shared in modern times by Yeats, Gide, Mann, Joyce, Hopkins (rather equivocally in this case), Lawrence, and Laforgue.

I said in the preface at the beginning of this book that "Song of Myself" is the kind of poem that arises from the native energies and dilemmas of life and is committed to the radical literary and cultural values of its time. All of Whitman's best writing arose in this way and was so committed. This test of a writer's immortality is always the telling one. It is decisive unless the times in which he wrote were themselves hopelessly second-rate, and Whitman's times were not. So that in the long run there can be no question that Whitman will live. But the question of how, or whether, he may be said to live for us, at a given moment in history, is always before us.

INDEX